C000084433

BURIED SEEDS

A CHEF'S JOURNEY

BURIED
SEEDS

A CHEF'S JOURNEY

THE STORY OF
VIKAS KHANNA

Karan Bellani

Now A Film By Andrei Severny

wisdom
tree

First published 2018
Cover Photo Credit: Omee Ganatra
Image on p 166 courtesy Vavci

ISBN 978-81-8328-497-4

Published by
Wisdom Tree
4779/23, Ansari Road
Darya Ganj, New Delhi-110 002
Ph.: 011-23247966/67/68
wisdomtreebooks@gmail.com

Printed in India

To
My dear grandparents
Shanti Devi and Tirathdas Bellani.
Your stories inspire poetry in me, every single day.

The walls, the mountains, the binds
Tall, and towering, and taut
But
The Spider
Tiny, and tender and thin
But
The Spider
Not troubled, not timid, never tired.

CONTENTS

Chef getting ready for work in New York City in 2010.

Chef on his way to shoot the promo of *Twist of Taste*, America.

On a day off, lounging on a scooter in Manhattan.

INTRODUCTION

Where there is ruin, there is hope for a treasure.

—Rumi

A man wearing a black sherwani was walking down the red carpet at the sixty-eighth Cannes Film Festival. Something he held in his hands had all his attention. No, it was not a trophy or a medal. It was a book like none other; one that he had nurtured for over a decade and was going to be a literary embodiment of the Indian culture. As the shutterbugs went on a clicking spree, little did they know about the amount of work Chef Vikas Khanna, and his team, had put into the making of *Utsav*, the first book ever to be launched at Cannes. Neither did they know that, moments ago, the man who was dressed up in front of them, had misplaced his socks and couldn't find a pair to wear with his outfit!

There was a time when I, too, had no clue about all the inside stories regarding this man. For me, like for most of us, Chef Vikas Khanna was a celebrity chef, a restaurateur with a Michelin-starred restaurant, a host and judge of multiple cookery shows, a bestselling author, a humble human, a unique filmmaker and much more. A lot had been written about him, but all of it talked about his glamorous side.

What happened when the cameras were not rolling? What did he talk about with the pillar of his strength and his inspiration—his mother? What kind of rapport did he share with his professors, mentors and batchmates of his alma mater in Manipal? How did he interact with new hotel management students who saw him as their inspiration? And, what inspired him to set off on a path that has seen him achieve things most can only dream of?

These questions and many more assailed my mind when I found that I had been hired to be a part of the food team of the cult food show, *MasterChef India*, to research the Indian cuisine for its fourth season, which had Chef Vikas on the panel of judges.

The journey of finding answers to my questions and discovering the man began at the boot-camp level of the show (screening of the contestants post the auditions). I remember the moment vividly. His back injury had flared up and he was facing difficulty climbing the stairs on the sets. I stood there, stunned at his grit and humility. He could have asked for shooting arrangements to be made in his vanity van, but he did not. He chose not to have any special treatment offered to him, and braved the stairs to the first floor to practise his tasks. That was not the end. His humble behaviour floored me when he saw me standing at the bottom of the staircase, walked up to me, shook my hand and introduced himself. I was taken aback. Of course, I knew who he was, but he had not assumed I did (I found out later that this was something he did with all the new people he met; he never assumed they knew him!). He asked me who I was. When he learnt I was a member of the food team, he told me how he considered it to be one of the most important parts of the show and insisted upon meeting the entire team even though he had to limp to the kitchen.

Until that handshake, the man had been an enigma for me, but after that moment, I knew that there was something inexplicably positive about him. I wanted to know more. And I did manage it during the time we worked together, whether it was while shooting for *MasterChef India* or during the crazy research and photo-shooting for *Utsav*, his culinary epic on India and during every other interaction we had when we were not working. Even when he was absent, remembering his speech at Harvard during the showcasing of *Utsav* for the students and professors there, stirred me. 'Where there is ruin, there is hope for a treasure,' he quoted the soul-stirring Persian poet, Rumi, as he spoke about how he had risen from extreme adversities and ruins to create a treasure like *Utsav*. Or the famous proverb he mentioned to me that had played an important role in his journey in America.

'They came to bury us, but they forgot that we were seeds.'

These words, on a small piece of paper, were always there with him in America and served as motivation each time someone tried to bury him and his dreams. The paper had become crumpled over the years, but it found a place on the top of the noticeboard in his office in New York. Pinned with an orange tack, along with one of his first kitchen tickets in New York, it has faded with time, but it stands vibrant and colourful in his heart to this very day. There are a few other things that give company to the kitchen ticket—a business card from his catering business in Amritsar, Lawrence Garden; pictures of him with his nieces, and a *mauli*, that was tied to his wrist by his *Biji*, Chef's grandmother, as she blessed him while he was leaving for America in the year 2000, to work, study, rise and pursue all other dreams that could not have been achieved in India. The lower part of the noticeboard changes every day, but these memories are a constant reminder of *Biji's* presence and her words, 'Make the family proud,' that she had whispered to him when he left that night to make his dreams come true.

Each story increased the respect I had for him and inspired me to do better myself. And that's when I knew that these stories and incidents we had shared together, things about him that had inspired me so much, needed to be told. The fire that burnt within him, and inspired him, needed to be spread far and wide.

At some point during our journey together, he went from being Chef Vikas Khanna to just 'Chef' for me. Sometimes, I also address him as *Veer* Ji, because he had slowly assumed the role of an elder brother in my life. But that form of address is only for special occasions, such as this moment when I'm writing this introduction.

This is for you, *Veer* Ji.

And for everyone who wants to know who Chef Vikas Khanna is and wants to see the Buried Seeds bloom.

FAILURE

The wound is a place where the light enters you.
—**Rumi**

Many memories are hidden away in the alleys of our minds. When they come knocking in the middle of the night in the form of a 'video' montage from the times we treasure, words fall short.

A few days before Thanksgiving in 2007, an unexpected person came to call on Chef's door. CBS News wanted to do a story with him on the occasion of the festival of gratitude. He remembers that 'they wanted to talk about an Indian meal and breads one could bake to render a multi-cultural flavour to the elaborate menus during the festival. I couldn't believe my ears. I couldn't believe that our "mango experiment" we had begun, soon after having worked with Gordon's team at *Purnima*, was paying off.'

Purnima was a restaurant in the heart of Manhattan, where tides turned after a stroke of luck in the form of Chef Gordon Ramsay.

Chef remembers that it was Friday, 6 April 2007, when he got a call from Gordon's office. They wanted an Indian chef who could work with him on his show, *Kitchen Nightmares*, and turn a restaurant around to make it successful.

'The call had come when I was busy with the morning shift at my restaurant, A *Spice Route*. They wanted me to go and meet Gordon and his team immediately, but I told them that one of my team members had not turned up that morning; I was handling the cash register while also working the tawa, where I was making *utthapams* and *dosas*. For a moment, I thought someone was playing a prank on me because why would *the* Gordon Ramsay want to meet me?'

The woman on phone started laughing because she couldn't believe that Chef was too busy to meet Gordon. But then she understood his predicament and it was agreed that he would go and see Gordon and his team at the London Hotel on 54th Street after his shift ended at 3:00 pm.

'After the call, I spent that entire morning thinking. I was very sceptical about being associated with a restaurant on the brink of collapse. I was also unsure about how my managerial style would blend with Gordon's, because of his reputation of being a tough taskmaster on his other show, *Hell's Kitchen*. But then it was Gordon Ramsay we were talking about, and if nothing else, I could not let go of this chance to meet him. So, I went to the London Hotel after my shift ended that afternoon. And, as they say, the rest is history. Over the discussion that went on for a few hours, I realised that Gordon was a very different person from what he appeared on television. He is someone who sets high standards for his team, but the standards that he sets for himself are even higher. After that discussion, I knew he would never ask me to do something he wouldn't do himself, and at *Purnima*, he was putting his personal reputation at stake.'

Chef agreed. Right on the next day, he was back at the sets of *Fox*, the channel that produced the show, for the preparation of the shoot. And on Sunday, the 8th, on the occasion of Easter, he was featured as a consultant chef on the show. His job was to devise and implement strategies along with Gordon, while bridging the cultural and language divides between the staff at *Purnima* and Gordon's team. This was one of the first places that saw him use all the experience he had harnessed over the years, right from the days in his childhood when *Biji* nurtured his talents, to the struggles in his initial days in America, which had brought out the tenacity in him.

His time there brings many happy memories back to him.

'*Purnima* was *Dillon's* when I joined the show, but Gordon wanted to change the name in an effort to change the restaurant's image. After discussion, I came up with the name *Purnima*, because my vision for the restaurant was to make it as beautiful as a full moon in splendour. In a short span, our efforts paid off and things started looking up.'

3 | Failure

But Gordon was not going to be happy with just that; he wanted the foundation that they had managed to lay along with Chef to turn into a beautiful piece of art they had envisioned. That was why he asked Chef if he would be willing to continue with his consulting services at *Purnima*.

'It was sort of a no-brainer because I had become attached to *Purnima* and the small team we had. I agreed, and soon after, the kitchen there became a testing ground for a lot of experiments. One of the things we tried, even though we knew it was not something the market was ready for, was a tasting menu. No one had tried it in an Indian restaurant before. But we wouldn't know if it would work or not until we actually tried it. So, we decided to start a three-course tasting menu called "The Feast of Mangoes". I remember we had priced it at USD 55 and the mango curries, purees and powders, the green-mango drinks, marinades and pickles, and of course the mango ice creams and shakes were lapped up by the crowds that stopped by before and after their shows at Broadway because we were very close to Times Square. Mango, for Indians, is not just a fruit; it is a very important part of our culture, and it seemed everyone in Manhattan wanted a taste of it. At the end of the meal, we also tried to give everybody a small piece of India to take to their homes in the form of a small packet of sour mango spice rub to "add some India to their food at home".'

Their efforts paid off. The show was aired on prime-time television across America and gained immense popularity.

Suddenly, Chef was a subject of discussion for thousands who watched him over dinner.

But then, sometimes, the montage also includes days we might not want to recall.

It was summer in 2009, and the days were longer than the white wintery days, but that particular day seemed to be exceptionally long. A huge lock stared at Chef as he stood at the entrance of *Purnima*—the entrance that would never be used to enter the restaurant again. The auctioning off of those 'worthless' pots and pans that had meant the world to him all those years brought back memories of experimenting with food and bringing the flavours of India to the people of New York. The same pots and pans had seen their moments of glory when they appeared on *Kitchen Nightmares* and had even been featured in the photo shoot of the food he had cooked for his sixth book that was being published by a publishing house, *Flavors First*. They were sacred to him—so much so that he remembered every scar and dent, the imperfect edges and the loose screws they had. But that day, as they were thrown around, it was all coming to an abrupt, jarring end.

'A lot of things in business are unforeseen. No one at *Purnima* could have predicted the call we received from the office next door. Overnight, we were asked to vacate the restaurant premises due to a property dispute with the owners. We tried everything and consulted many lawyers, but all of them told us the same thing: we had no chance against the big corporations we were up against. We were advised to begin preparing for the inevitable end. Some days later, the owners had put me in charge of what used to be our home to clear everything out. I was watching over the proceedings with Sammy, the supervisor of the building, when I saw the auctioneers empty the entire restaurant. At that moment, some coins and currency notes fell out from the cash register. I picked the money up and gave it to Sammy. I told him it was *Purnima's* last earning and I wanted him to have it for his little daughter. Soon after, when everything had been moved out, as I stood in the empty space, the blank walls reminded me of the movie, *You've Got Mail*, where Meg Ryan feels like a child when she enters her store for one last time. The paisley tapestry with various spiritual symbols, the yellow walls, which were a reminder of turmeric and mangoes from back home, the framed picture of New Delhi's Red Fort on the wall that kept a watchful eye on all of us, and even the intricate woodwork—everything had disappeared in the blink of an eye. And then there was that final lock on the door.'

The lock told him the story that had repeated itself many times over—of the days when his restaurant, *Tandoor Palace*, didn't survive despite being renamed as *A Spice Route*, or the losses that he had to incur while running his catering business, Flavors and Feasts, which led to its shutdown, and even the cooking classes, 'Sanskrit Culinary Arts', that had many no-shows even after people had registered—all of it was coming back in that one infinite moment and the days of being broke were staring back at him.

But each cloud has a silver lining. While his ventures in the past had been unsuccessful, they had helped in building on the foundation that had been laid during his days in India.

Tandoor Palace had been ailing before Chef had joined hands with the owners to revive it. They were faced with a unique challenge there—the hole-in-the-wall restaurant was frequented by the employees of Wall Street, which meant good business for five days of the week, but weekends were tough. They even tried to rename the restaurant to *A Spice Route* to make it feature higher on the alphabetical lists of websites that potential clients frequented before ordering online or calling in for deliveries. But all of it was only delaying the inevitable, and eventually they were forced to shut down.

While the pain of not being able to save *Tandoor Palace* was not easy to cope with, it was his work and ingenuity there that was noticed and led to meeting Gordon. Coincidentally, the shutters were downed in the same week as Chef was featured on *Kitchen Nightmares*.

Among the thousands who watched Chef on *Kitchen Nightmares*, there were many Indian restaurateurs too. Intense discussions followed with some of them, spread over countless days that turned into weeks, months and years.

Slowly but steadily, a dream that had been nebulous in Chef's mind for many years, began to take form. And three-and-a-half years after he was featured on prime-time television for the first time in his life, it was born in the form of a restaurant in the Flatiron district of Manhattan on

2 December 2010. It was everything that Chef had wanted his restaurant to be.

'It was not easy, especially after how we had been forced to end things at *Purnima*. But during my time there, there was one person who helped me turn my vision into reality—Andrew Blackmore. He had been working at *Purnima* from the time it was *Dillon's* and he was the one who wrote to Gordon's team to ask them for help. He wanted them to come and help turn the restaurant around. That is the reason why he understood my pain when *Purnima* had to be shut down. He also knew exactly what I wanted to do at my own restaurant. He did not work anywhere else during the period between the shutting down of *Purnima* and the birth of *Junoon*, because he knew about the "big dream". I was scared, but I could not show that on my face whenever I met him. But somehow, he understood and he was always there. Right from the day *Junoon* was born, he managed it and helped me run the kitchen.

'Andrew used to say, "You have to have the imagination to believe it is possible to come here to America and work your way up from the very bottom."'

It was the power of this imagination that helped tide him over many difficult periods.

Whether it is with his electric moves on the basketball court, or his powerful words off it, Michael Jordan has inspired millions over the years, and he continues to do so. He once said, 'I've failed over and over in my life and that is why I succeed.' These words strike a chord with Chef each time he suffers from setbacks and failures.

Inspired by Jordan, Chef often repeats them: 'I've failed many times. Life has hit me in the gut over and over. And that is why I succeed. These failures have acted like milestones.'

Sarina D'Silva Menezes, one of Chef's seniors and friends at his alma mater, Welcomgroup Graduate School of Hotel Administration (WGSHA), feels that 'many times, failure is as much of a milestone in life as is success; it teaches humility. Despite all the success, Vikas is still the same as he was during college. His humility touches every person he meets.'

Sarina was visiting Manipal, a small city nestled in the hills of the southern Indian state of Karnataka, the place where her journey had started many years ago. It was a day similar to that moment when a similar journey was starting for a new batch of students of WGSHA in 2016. After she had spoken at the induction ceremony, held every year to help the new students feel at home in their new college, it was time for yet another part of the ceremony that was held every year.

For the past few years, a particular call during this induction ceremony had shaped up to become a ritual; a ritual that everyone at the college, whether it is the senior students, or the new joiners, and even the professors await every year—a Skype call of the new batch with Chef.

Being a part of these induction ceremonies every year takes Chef back to the days when he was in Manipal.

'During a similar induction ceremony, many years ago, another person who has been an integral part of my journey was present—Professor YG Tharakan.'

It was in 1991 when the nineteen-year-old boy, Viku, had set out from Amritsar telling everyone that he would return only after becoming a chef in Manipal. Much before the induction ceremony, the interview was an important step where every student had to prove his or her mettle.

'Everyone was speaking in the group discussion that was a part of the interview process. My English was so bad that I got scared and ran away.'

The interviews were being carried out in New Delhi. Chef was staying with Surinder *Bua* in Noida, one of the satellite cities of the capital. Leaving the group discussion, he returned to his aunt but he did not have it in him to speak to her about what had happened. Eventually, the next day, he did speak to her and told her what had happened.

'I told her I didn't stay for the group discussion because I would have failed. She said that failure was a possibility but, if I did not go back, I would have definitely failed. So, I went back and called the principal of WGSHA, Professor Sundresh Prasad. I started explaining what had gone wrong and why I had run away. I was so worked up that I was talking to him in Punjabi. I went on repeating that everyone was better than me and that was the case everywhere.'

Principal Prasad had no clue about who the wailing boy on the phone was, but he understood through all the crying and loud Punjabi that he was someone who had appeared for an interview and wanted to study at WGSHA. So, he went down with Professor Tharakan, the vice principal of WGSHA at that time, to try and figure out what was going on.

Chef has a firm belief which he often voices, 'The biggest disability is the inability to see ability.'

That day, Principal Prasad and Professor Tharakan saw that the boy who had come to them didn't speak English or even proper Hindi. But what they did see was enough for their experienced eyes. He spoke about food and hospitality from his heart. They looked beyond the surface and decided to give the boy a chance. They hadn't the slightest inkling that the boy they were putting their trust in was going to embark upon a journey that would take him from being Viku to a globally-respected chef.

But much before the dreams turned into reality, many harsh truths were waiting for him.

It wasn't smooth sailing at the college as he struggled with things like the language barrier, the fact that he was never good with technology, and even his shy demeanour. He was not comfortable with numbers. It led to him being failed in a project in the fifth semester where he had to prepare the financial-viability and market-feasibility report for a five-star hotel. And sometimes, despite his efforts, it was tough to keep up with the home assignments because he was inclined towards gaining practical experience and learning the local cuisines by visiting the homes of the staff members.

And all of it piled up in the end as, even after graduating from WGSHA in the summer of 1994 with a great deal of knowledge about running the hospitality business, as well as local cuisines, he was not hired by ITC, the hotel that was affiliated with his college. But he was not ready to look at it as a failure. His tenacity saw him train at reputed hotels like Leela Kempinski, Mumbai; Taj, Delhi; Soaltee Oberoi, Kathmandu; and Sea Rock Sheraton, Mumbai. And soon after being trained at all these hallowed institutions, ITC too reversed their decision and gave him an opportunity to sharpen his skills at the ITC Mughal Sheraton in Agra.

He worked at Leela for three years, but there was a constant calling in his heart that he knew he had to answer.

'Not being hired by ITC turned out to be a blessing in disguise. I got to learn a lot at the Leela property in Mumbai. I also realised that I had to bring what I had learnt over the years in college and then in Leela, to my home, Amritsar, because, if I did not do that, it wouldn't be right. My mother had been running the business we had started before I went to Manipal, all by herself. I had to go back.'

For Chef, knowing his strengths, dreaming, and then focusing on his dreams and guarding them like a tigress guards her cubs—and persisting, no matter what hurdles and failures came his way—was something taught to him right from his childhood, and it continues every day, at each and every step of his life.

'I feel destiny had a part to play in all my ventures that

were not successful. Because had Lawrence Garden been successful, I would never have thought of moving to America. And had my cooking classes and the catering business not shut down, I would not have tried doubly hard to succeed. And had *Purnima* (which means a full moon) not shut down and become an eclipse, maybe the next chapter would not have been born out of the dark nights that had come to stay in my life. Had I succeeded at the first thing I tried, I would have never thought of other possibilities to improve myself.'

THE FAMILY OF DREAM CATCHERS

For teaching us that falling only makes us stronger.
Thank you, Mom.
—A P&G Commercial for Sochi 2014
Olympic Winter Games

It was a bright day in the summer of 2016. SUVs, bikes, 4x4s, all lined up at the starting line as they waited for the 500-kilometre madness through the Himalayas to begin. Among that bunch of powerful, modified automobiles, there was a tiny, white hatchback, which had a woman at its helm. She was one of the few women participating, but there was one important difference—she was seventy.

'You know that spark all of us have? We try and nurture it in our family. But then the gust of wind that lights a spark can also extinguish it,' Nishant Khanna, Chef Vikas Khanna's elder brother, said while talking about their mother, Mrs

Bindu Khanna and her participation in the Himalayan rally. The Iron Lady, as she is known among her family and friends, drives herself around in the busy lanes of Amritsar, managing various aspects of the family's businesses. And she even knows how to fly a plane! But ever since the passing of her husband, Davinder Khanna, on 31 January 2015, the family observed that her spirits were low. They knew they needed to encourage her to pursue something that would reignite the spark in her, and that was when they persuaded her to go after one of her cherished dreams—to take part in a car rally! She participated with a small hatchback, and not a big, powerful SUV. Not only did she finish the race, she got a standing ovation from all the participants, audience, and the organisers alike!

But this was not the first time that one of the family members had been encouraged by the family to follow his/her dream.

In the summer of 1991, soon after finishing high school with subjects that would help him opt for engineering in college, Chef had visited Mumbai to meet his elder brother. Nishant, an engineer, was working with a multinational company in Mumbai. The duo sat in a dimly-lit room in Nishant's home discussing life. Chef had submitted an application for admission in an engineering college and it had been accepted, but his heart wasn't in it.

A few days before visiting Mumbai, Chef was invited to Delhi to pay a visit to Baboo *Chacha,* his uncle. While he was in Delhi, his uncle took him to the midnight buffet at *Pavilion,* the coffee shop of the Maurya Sheraton Hotel. The daily routine surrounding food at their home, back in Amritsar, was almost like a sacred ritual full of love for him, and that helped him want to make food his life in the future, but what he saw at the hotel's buffet was something entirely different.

Chef remembers, 'The food there was like art. I went down on my knees and cried like a baby.'

The variety of carefully sculpted works opened up his imagination and dreams. Baboo *Chacha* knew about Chef's passion for food, and he was the first person in the family to encourage Chef to seek admission at a hotel management institute. Baboo *Chacha* was a huge fan of the quality and workmanship of the food at Maurya Sheraton, a part of the ITC Group, that he had shown to Chef at the midnight buffet. And that was the reason why he encouraged Chef to go to Manipal's WGSHA to pursue his dreams.

Sometimes we need a nudge as we stand at the precipice while pursuing our dreams. That is what happened that night in Mumbai as the elder brother nudged the younger brother to pursue his dreams of making a career in the hospitality industry, which had come alive sometime during that buffet. It was followed by a discussion about the decision with their parents and younger sister, Radhika.

Ever since his boyhood, Chef has been known as Viku amongst family and friends. So much so that if he is addressed as 'Chef Vikas' in front of them, the words take a few seconds to register. But they've always believed in the power of dreams.

The famous quote by Albert Einstein, 'Everyone is a genius, but if you judge a fish by its ability to climb a tree, it will live its whole life believing that it is stupid,' is deeply instilled in the family.

After discussions over dinners that the family ensured were shared together, and the drives around the city that followed them, the decision to set sail in the direction of the dreams had been taken.

'*Biji* taught me how to dream,' Chef often says.

Right from the beginning, *Biji* had been a nurturer of dreams in his life. Generally, in Indian households, while the parents are busy providing for the family and running the household, the grandparents take up the responsibility of laying the foundation of culture and values in the lives of their grandchildren. The mischief, laughter and the stories that the children share with the grandparents often stay with them through their lifetime. Chef was born with misaligned feet and couldn't run due to the heavy shoes he had to wear, which is why he spent most of his time indoors with *Biji*. 'The rituals we used to follow on special days like our birthdays are followed even today, even if we are not there,' he remembers fondly. Even on routine days, the hot rotis made on the old, black tawa were a symbol of continuity that had been passed down in the family for generations. The bond between them that developed during these difficult times of Chef's boyhood makes his face light up even today as he speaks about her, and even the mention of her name makes him feel safe.

One day, he got back from school and noticed that the kitchen that was normally kept spic-and-span by *Biji* was in a mess. He instantly knew that something was wrong. When he checked on her, he found that she was sick and in her bed. The kitchen was her haven and she took pride in keeping it clean. He was only seven and didn't know much about cooking, but that was not going to deter him from trying to make her happy. 'She does it every day. I can definitely do it once,' he thought, as he cleaned the place and decided to make chai for her. The joy in her eyes as he placed the pot of dark, almost-burnt chai with milk on the side gave him the motivation to take more steps. He made yellow *masoor dal* next. Right after *Biji* recovered, the duo began their kitchen adventures.

'I knew *Biji* was there, looking after me silently as I learnt cooking.'

He used to observe her clockwork routine. It started much before he woke up and rushed to school. The mornings, after the children left, were usually occupied with buying fresh vegetables and other groceries. And once the three siblings returned from school, *Biji* and Chef's mother used to feed them and take a nap for an hour after that. After the nap, when Chef had *Biji* all to himself is when he got to observe her going about her cooking rituals, and gained from her knowledge she would share with her enthusiastic grandson. Her experienced, wrinkled hands used to work effortlessly through the sorting, rinsing and chopping. It was as if the kitchen was under her spell and that magic rubbed off on him as well.

Slowly, the new-found independence that had been set off by a messy kitchen laid the foundation of a dream that became his life.

While *Biji* stood for learning, comfort and nurturing in Chef's life, *Bauji* brought the colours of art and creativity into his life. He fondly calls *Bauji* 'the poet of the family'. *Bauji*, like many Indian grandparents, taught him and his siblings about Indian culture over countless hours of watching the Indian epics, *Ramayana* and *Mahabharata* on television. And when he discussed politics with his friends, he never discouraged his grandchildren from soaking in the intense debates that the adults were often involved in. These were often followed by recitals of poetry by some of the renowned Urdu poets like Mirza Ghalib, Rumi and Faiz, and they gave birth to the poet in Chef.

Ironically, this poet was given a shot of encouragement on one of the saddest days in his life. *Bauji* had passed away. It was the first time that he had seen a death in the family. But instead of grieving and chanting the traditional words, he decided to honour his grandfather by playing his favourite Ghalib poetry on an old tape recorder they had. 'Papa didn't stop me. Somehow, he always understood me and knew why I was doing something that might have seemed illogical to others. He knew how much I had loved *Bauji* and how I was honouring him with his favourite words that echoed through the house.'

Hui muddat Ghalib mar gaya par yaad aata hai,
Woh har ek baat pe kehta,
Ki yun hota toh kya hota?

It has been a while since my friend, Ghalib,
passed away, but he comes to mind often,
At every turn he would say,
What would have happened had things been this way?

According to Indian mythology, Lord Shiva, the Hindu God of Destruction, narrated a story to his wife, Goddess Parvati, in the Amarnath Cave or the Cave of Immortality. It is believed that the story contained the secret to immortality. Anyone who heard the entire tale became immortal. At some point during the narration, Goddess Parvati fell asleep, but there were a couple of pigeons in the cave that heard the entire story and, as a result, became immortal.

At some point during the recitals of the poems, songs and the discussions, the seeds had been sown in Chef's mind. That day, a poet had died, but he had passed on his legacy to the 'pigeon' in his home.

The rich cultural legacy that had been passed on to him by his grandparents had received constant nurturing from his parents. His mother, who is another pillar of strength in his life, had fought battles with and for him right from the beginning. On 14 November 1971, when he was born with misaligned feet, the doctors told her that her son would never be able to walk or run like a normal child. But nothing stopped her from fighting nature—not the pessimism of the doctors, not the war that broke out that year and not even the financial troubles that the family faced. Amritsar, close to the border India shares with Pakistan, was the city where Chef had been born and raised. Within a few days of his birth, war had broken out, but that did not deter his mother one bit from doing what was needed. She got him operated in Delhi in the middle of the war, and then ensured that he wore special shoes with braces despite the crisis the family was facing. She managed to save money and got him new shoes each time his fast-growing feet outgrew them, even though they cost almost five times the normal shoes. She stood by him each time a jibe was directed at him by the other students in his class.

In the summer of 1984, when he ran freely through Company Bagh near their home in Amritsar for the first time in his life, she was right there, standing by him.

There were times when Chef's parents felt a little sceptical about him pursuing his dreams in the hospitality industry. In those years, a career in it was not seen on par with traditional choices like Medicine or Engineering, or Chartered Accountancy. But they kept their thoughts to themselves and encouraged him instead of cutting off his wings. They also encouraged his inclination towards other forms of art like sculpting, sketching and painting.

'Papa taught us discipline, but he also gave us independence and never stopped us from pursuing our interests,' he says.

The backyard of Chef's house was his workshop where he let his imagination free in the form of various clay and mud statues. The statues, some finished, some incomplete, and some of the naughty ones playing hide-and-seek, peeped from the nooks and crannies, giving fresh impetus to Chef's young mind each time he saw them. When he was exploring other forms of art, he saw some sketches and paintings by various European masters like Michelangelo, Picasso, Da Vinci and Van Gogh in some magazines he bought from the scrap market. The masters inspired him and he started making a sketch that changed his life forever. The teenaged boy in the company of the masters gave birth to a sketch of a nude woman. But, in the conservative Khanna household, while he had been encouraged to pursue all forms of art, this was the tipping point that led to complete mayhem. And that was when Chef's aunt, Sushma *Didi* as he fondly calls her, stepped in. During her travels to Europe and other parts of the Western world, she had seen art in various forms and knew how important it was for it to be given freedom to prosper.

'Don't kill the artist in him,' she told the family as she addressed their concerns.

They understood her and there was no looking back for Chef. Sushma *Didi* sold him dreams and he bought them. She told him about five-star hotels across the world.

'One day I will own a five-star hotel,' he proclaimed to her in Punjabi. In Punjabi slang, the word 'hotel' is often used as a substitute for a restaurant.

The disability with which he was born had set him apart from the crowd literally as well as figuratively, because, in his own words, 'I could cook and they could not.' But instead of weighing him down, it had seen him set out on a journey ever since the day he had cooked his first meal—the yellow *masoor dal*. And now the journey had a new, distinct direction.

'You're given one little spark of madness. You mustn't lose it.' These words of Robin Williams come to mind when one thinks about how the culinary world could have lost someone who has redefined the word 'chef', had that spark not been nurtured by the family of dream catchers, and extinguished somewhere in the journey of engineering that nearly began.

BITTER GOURDS, MOPEDS AND FRIENDS

Be with those who help your being.
—**Rumi**

What is common between a pack of handsome lions and gorgeous lionesses, lounging in the Savannah; a group of green parrots sitting on an electric wire near your home; and a bunch of little schoolchildren, dressed in their dirt-stained uniforms, walking hand-in-hand?

It is the bond of companionship. We may call it kinship, brotherhood or friendship, but the string of love ties all of them together. For years and years, through pranks and hardships, and through sickness and health, somehow, everything feels right with the words 'I've got your back', whether spoken through the lips or the eyes.

Dr Kapil Mohindru is a well-known medical practitioner in Amritsar. But for Chef he is Kapil, and for Kapil he is Viku, a friend from his boyhood days who he used to cycle with to school. And sometimes, when Chef's mother, Bindu Aunty, as she is known to almost everyone outside the family, was not able to wake little Viku up since she would be busy with preparing the lunch boxes for her children, it was Kapil's duty to wake him up. The duty also included shouting at him if he found Viku still sleeping, blissfully unaware that they were terribly late for school.

When he met Kapil in the fifth grade at St Francis School, Viku was a frail boy, recovering from the illness he was born with. His legs were gaining new strength each day, but he was not able to play or run a lot like the other kids, and that made him the subject of more jibes. He never retaliated or spoke much, but whenever he did, most of the words were directed at Kapil.

But he had one outlet and that was art. He would make various clay sculptures and paintings, spending hours of his time in the backyard of their house, lost in his own world. And he found immense pleasure in sharing the works of his imagination with Kapil. The two boys were each other's confidantes and did everything together, right from sharing their food to getting into trouble. Like all boys their age, they had their share of pin-pricks, giggles and cycling around. But when they were caught doing some mischief, it was Viku's responsibility to bail them out because, somehow, he always managed to be in the good books of the teachers.

Kapil remembers that, 'His mischievous and innocent smile definitely helped him, but I think Viku had emotional strength and strong empathy right from his childhood. Maybe it was because he had been through a lot right from the beginning. He knew the value of human relationships. I still remember the countless times when he spent whatever little pocket money that he got on eating ice cream and chaat with me. He spent it all. When he needed something, he had no problem with borrowing it.'

On one such occasion when Viku needed new shoes to go for a friend's birthday party, he did not have any money. But that did not deter him from finding an ingenious solution—he borrowed his grandfather's shoes lying idle and stuffed them with cotton to make them fit his small feet. And when he returned them, he forgot to remove the cotton.

'*Bauji* was angry at Viku because his feet were not fitting into his own shoes. He thought one of the children in the house had pulled a prank on him.'

Kapil and Viku cycled to school till the tenth grade. They used their cycles to go everywhere else too, whether it was to birthday parties of the other children or the playground and for their endless pursuits of mischief and snacking.

'I did not realise then, but he used to cycle everywhere with me despite being weak because I had a bicycle,' Kapil mentioned. 'And on one occasion our classmates, some of whom had mopeds, asked Viku to go for a ride with them because he had helped them out with the teachers at school. He refused. He didn't say anything to me, but I knew that he had done that because they hadn't asked me to come along and he didn't want to leave me behind on my bicycle.'

But when Kapil shared these memories with his daughters, who were used to seeing Chef on television, they refused to believe they were buddies during their childhood because they had never seen Chef visit their home.

Chef's travels and the fact that he now lives in New York City sometimes makes it tough for him to spend much time in India. But recently, when he visited Amritsar, he made it a point to go to Kapil's home without informing him in advance. He wanted to surprise Kapil and his family and a plan to cook for them was also brewing in his mind. When he found out that the only vegetable they had in the house was bitter gourd, he cooked it for them, much to the chagrin of the young ones. They did not want to eat something that was that bitter, whether it was made by Chef, their mother, or anyone else. But maybe it was the bond of childhood that added that extra bit of sweetness to even something like bitter gourd, which was lapped up by the family after their initial scepticism subsided.

'He might be far in terms of the distance, but incidents like these show me that no matter where he has reached, he is still the same Viku he was when we met for the first time.'

Another partner-in-crime that Chef had in his childhood was his younger sister, Radhika.

Radhika understood him well. Since she was the youngest in the family, the mischievous side of Chef used to come out in front of her. Along with the pranks, she was his companion in another realm of creative pursuits—street plays and dancing. The duo was responsible for organising plays and dance performances during various festivities and celebrations in their neighbourhood as well as their school and, sometimes, it was at the cost of studies and homework.

Radhika remembers that 'nothing in Viku's and my school bags changed because, right after school, we used to drop our bags and even without changing out of our uniforms, we would rush off to practise for the plays and dances that we were always organising and participating in near our home.'

And every time the brother-sister duo got caught in fights with their friends, it was the responsibility of their elder brother, Nishant, to broker peace and bail them out.

These friendships forged during his childhood have stayed with Chef, but some new bonds were also forged to help him through the rigours of the new phases in his life, whether it was during his challenges in Manipal or during the adventures that he embarked upon in America, and then, during the world of spotlights and short-lived memories.

One of the people that became his closest friends during the years of study at Manipal's WGSHA was Pallav Baruah.

Professor YG Tharakan, who was the vice-principal at the college, was also the person in charge of the hostel arrangements. He remembers, 'Pallav, Shanthasheela and Parminder were Vikas's roommates in the three years of college. But for some reason Vikas took Pallav under his wing.'

There were many occasions when he was punished because of Pallav, but that did not affect their friendship. And sometimes, they indulged in mischief together.

In fact, Professor Tharakan feels Chef pushed himself harder to ensure that the scrutiny he was subjected to due to his proximity with Pallav did not affect his studies.

Another friend who came into Chef's life at a challenging time was Jason DiTullio, a chiropractor based in New York. He was one of the first people Chef became friends with. Jason says, 'I met him when I went to *Salaam Bombay* for a Sunday brunch. Vikas had moved to New York recently and when we spoke, we realised that we had nothing in common. Maybe that is why the conversations were so interesting.'

And even when he is not able to meet his friends regularly due to his busy schedule, travelling across the world, he has a way of maintaining friendships with those who were there for him in the hour of need.

One such friend Chef addresses as his 'Jewish Mother' is Arlyn Blake. Arlyn is an award-winning writer, who has been associated with the James Beard Foundation for more than a decade. She was the one who introduced Chef to the realm where food meets the glitterati of the world after they met for the first time in her James Beard House in the spring of 2004.

'Shining stars in a row. This is how I think of my kind of "once a day/once a decade" occasions with Vikas,' she says.

'In this busy world, we fought hard not to lose touch, and I was always honoured to be included in all the heart-warming, small celebrations of his accomplishments. He has a way of honouring the person he is with, but truly, it is that person who has the pleasure of his friendship. I do not have any anecdotes, but I do have lasting memories of quiet breakfasts where dreams were discussed and love was shared.

'Vikas is a very, very special young friend. Right from the day we met at my office, I was hooked and remain a dedicated mentor and cheerleader.'

Then there are times when he goes straight from the high arc lights of the events he hosts to some place in the middle of nowhere just because he has to celebrate the birthday of a friend. And sometimes he lands up at a friend's house, like he did at Jalal Shaikh's. Chef has known Jalal ever since he began his *MasterChef India* journey. For him, *MasterChef* is incomplete without Jalal, and without the taste of the biryani made by Jalal's mother he has whenever he gets to visit them after wrapping up the hectic shooting in Mumbai.

And these are things that his friends remember—and probably will forever.

Manisha Singh who works with Smile Foundation, the charity Chef is associated with, feels, 'Vikas walks into the life of the people who are close to him. And this also includes the lives of the extended families of these people. I remember my mother-in-law, who lives in Benaras, has seen Vikas only once in person, but she has seen me interact with him over the phone and such is the connection that in 2012, when he was in India during summers, she sent a box of mangoes from her farm for him and his family in Amritsar. And this is what makes him special.'

For Chef, there is only one truth that was taught to him by *Biji*: 'Friendship is not just one thing, it is a sum total of many small things.'

THANK YOU, JOHN

You may say I'm a dreamer, but I'm not the only one.
—John Lennon

A man with a dream can move mountains. And the power of one dream—the dream of taking Indian food to the world in its true form—made Chef uproot himself from Amritsar, on the night of 2 December 2000.

His elder niece, Ojasvi, was barely a few months old. Chef's mother was driving him to the railway station in Amritsar so that he could commence the first leg of his long journey to America—take a train to Delhi. But the daunting journey was the last thing on his mind as his eyes were glued to the little fingers of Ojasvi holding his hand as she slept in his lap.

'I've never held anything so precious in my hands. Handing the sleeping ball back to her mother was one of the most difficult things I've ever done in my life.'

As he handed her over and bade farewell to his family, *Biji* tied a *mauli* around his wrist while blessing him. Everyone knew that the farewell was difficult for the closely-knit Khanna household, but the journey that lay ahead for Chef was going to be far more so.

After moving to America, within a few days, Chef was broke. He had to sustain himself by doing many things—dishwashing, taking care of pets and houses, delivering produce and many similar odd jobs.

One of the many things he did was hand out flyers, standing in front of one of the entrances to Central Park. One evening, when he was standing near the West 72nd Street entrance, something told him to enter.

While walking through the park, he stumbled upon something he remembers vividly to this day. It was a black-and-white mosaic.

The circular artwork made up of a single word, 'Imagine', attracted thousands of tourists every day, and they let their imagination run as they decorated it with roses and orchids to pay homage to John Lennon.

Imagine no possessions
I wonder if you can
No need for greed or hunger
A brotherhood of man
Imagine all the people sharing all the world

When he saw this memorial dedicated to John Lennon, the words of his song, *Imagine,* came to his mind. Instantly, he was reminded of the image of himself he had seen in the mirror a few years ago where he was struggling to run Lawrence Garden and keeping it afloat despite the low margins. In that moment he knew that he did not want to continue struggling in America too and see himself grow old earning USD 14 per shift. That was not what he had come to do in America. The power of his dreams, the power of the imagination of the Americans that had propelled them to the moon and inspired many others, and the words of the song combined to give birth to Captain Imagination in his mind.

'What separates Manhattan from Queens is not a tunnel or a bridge, but imagination. That is the difference between the people who live and work there, and everywhere else in the world, and I wanted to move to "this island of imagination". I wanted to move there and call it my second home, my home away from home.'

Chef had always believed that the word Inspiration comes before Imagination. 'You need to be inspired to imagine,' is what he says often. That day he was inspired all over again. So much so that even today, whenever he is seeking inspiration, one of the places he goes to is that very spot where he connected with Lennon.

And speaking of places where Chef goes to feel inspired, anything said about Amritsar is too little. The city has a vibe that can only be felt and revelled in. Right from the time when you set your first foot on the grounds of this holy city (it is home to one of the most revered sites for the Sikh community of India, the Golden Temple), something inexplicable brings a smile to your face. Maybe it is the sight of the tractors with their baby trolleys in tow—an inseparable part of the agricultural industry; or maybe it is the aroma of delicious food in almost every nook and cranny; or perhaps it is the holy chanting of the Golden Temple that resonates in almost all the homes, whether big or small. But for Chef, along with all the love the city has to offer, it is also home to what is inspiration personified for him—his mother.

Right from his childhood, his family has been his backbone that has given him strength in all his endeavours. The simple yet exquisite food cooked at home by *Biji* and his mother had inspired him for life. And this inspiration was strengthened each time he visited the Golden Temple and helped in the cooking at the langar, the free community kitchen run there. Even today, whenever he visits the city, he makes it a point to visit the temple to eat prasad, the blessed food at the langar, and cook too, even if only for some time. And these visits are interspersed with visits to his favourite childhood haunts too—his quaint home with a green door, where he was born and raised; the narrow alleys which can barely accommodate one car, but were wide enough for him, his sister, Radhika, and their friends to organise plays and dance-offs; the Company Bagh which symbolised freedom for him in more ways than one; the homes of his extended family and childhood friends which are full of sumptuous goodies each time he visits them; and even visits to the schools where he studied to meet the teachers and see the winding passageways.

He had left a part of him behind at his home in Amritsar, but on that day of spring in New York City, a new friendship was shaping up. Soon enough, John started helping Chef find a slow, peaceful haven of imagination in the middle of the noises and chaos of the urban sprawl. As he walked through the green lungs of New York, he reminisced about the time he spent with his family and friends in Company Bagh.

All the worries were left far behind.

Thank you, John.

THE WINGS OF FAITH

Faith is the knowledge within the heart, beyond the reach of proof.
—Kahlil Gibran

A mother nurtures her child as a part of her own body for many months, an architect invests years of his life connecting two ends of the abyss, and the sea keeps sending waves to the shore to show its eternal love.

We don't know what the future holds; we don't know if what we are planning and dreaming about, will happen or not. But despite that, we continue to plan, and dream, and hope, and we base it all on faith.

'I had gone through many failed ventures and I had been broke on multiple occasions. I was unemployed many times, but I had managed to keep moving. However, after *Purnima* shut down in the summer of the year 2009, I was on the verge of giving up. Somebody even commented that the "poster boy" of Indian food was gone. I did not care about any of that because I was, and am, just a cook. That was all I had always wanted to do. But America is a country where people put out signs in front of their establishments when they are out of business. Failing is an option in America, because no one cares if you fail. People look to see if the ones who have failed can rise again. I had never imagined how the selling of all the equipment at *Purnima* would make me feel. I didn't know if I could rise again. I had opened the doors of the restaurant at 6:00 in the morning, but instead of preparing for service after flipping the sign at the entrance to say that we were "open for business", that day I let the sign continue to say "closed for business". I got busy packing the utensils and bowls and glasses. We had to make them ready to be transported. By 10:00 am, everything was gone.'

The first time a restaurant is empty is when it is being built on the foundation of countless dreams and fistfuls of hope. But then there is yet another time, the day when the restaurant is shutting down; the day when it appears like a house which has been robbed of all its children, and along with them, the joy and laughter. The empty space where *Purnima* used to be was screaming to Chef and telling him how transient everything was.

But even after all that he had gone through that day, something told Chef to hang on.

And it didn't take long for the universe to reveal its plans.

As he was locking the door, he got a call from Tashi Chodron, whom he had met while hosting events at the Rubin Museum of Art (RMA) in New York. She was also the creator of a blog called 'Voices of Tibet'. On her blog, and during the conversations with Chef, she had often spoken about Tibetan culture, but on that particular day, she had called to ask him if he wanted to meet His Holiness the Dalai Lama, who was visiting New York City.

'I started to tell her that I was locking up *Purnima* forever but, before I could, she said she was planning to bring His Holiness to Rubin Museum of Art on his next visit. That was when I told her what had happened that morning. She said she could sense that something was wrong. She asked me if I wanted to meet His Holiness because she knew that I'd always been a follower of the legend. But that day I turned her offer down because I was in no state to go anywhere.'

But despite what Chef said, Tashi told him that His Holiness was scheduled to speak at the Beacon Theatre on 74th and Broadway Street in Manhattan, the next day, 4 May 2009, and that he would be welcome if he wanted to visit. Chef declined once again and went straight home, oblivious to the sounds of the bustling city as the sounds in mind drowned everything else. A troubled night filled with nightmares followed. When he woke up, it was morning. His body was used to waking up early, given his routine at *Purnima*, and when he noticed the clock that day, he realised that it was 7:45 am. Panic struck as he rushed to get ready for work, but while he was doing that he realised there was no workplace to go to. The force of habit had made him forget that the 'full moon' of his life had been eclipsed. He decided to take a walk to *Purnima* to press his mind to believe what it was refusing to acknowledge.

And after he had a long look at the lock on the doors of his beloved restaurant, he continued walking down the street.

'I didn't realise that while walking I had crossed Central Park South. A little while later when I looked up, I was at the 74th and Broadway Street. I was in denial. The shock of *Purnima* having shut down had still not sunk in, but I was right at the place where I was supposed to be. So I thought of calling Tashi. When I pulled my phone out, I realised the battery was about to die because I had gone to bed without bothering to charge it. I called Tashi. As soon as I had told her I was at the Beacon Theatre, the phone died. I went searching for her to the reception and found her there looking for me. She took me through this long corridor that led to the auditorium where His Holiness was going to speak. There were hundreds of people standing on both the sides of the corridor with their heads bowed. We, too, stood in the queue while we waited, and then one of the most unbelievable things happened. While entering the hall, His Holiness touched my forehead and left without saying a word. What left me dumbstruck was that he didn't touch anyone else's head. I knew it was a sign. I thought of staying for the lecture, but I was worried that someone might try to call me and my phone was discharged. I realised at that time that all that had happened till the day before had been erased and I was getting a brand new chance to write a new chapter in life.'

The auditorium was packed. Chef didn't get a chance to sit, but that didn't matter because the words of His Holiness had him captivated.

His Holiness began talking. 'America is a country where the life and comforts are so evolved that the thing that people start fearing the most is death. They get comfortable with their lives and think that everything is planned and laid out for them. They start fearing death more than the loneliness, and even fear that nobody loves them. But if you look closely at the spectrum of time and space, there is no such thing as death. Things only change form. If they are not broken and destroyed, change won't be possible. But then change is always possible. If seeds lie in a farm for years, hidden away somewhere in dust, one might think they have no life left in them, but at the right moment, change happens and they evolve from being "dead" to new saplings full of life and hope.'

And the sign repeated itself when that same night, soon after the event had ended at the Beacon Theatre, a representative of His Holiness asked Chef if he wanted to see the spiritual leader again at an event called *Thank You, India,* being hosted at the Waldorf Astoria the next day, 5 May 2009.

'My mother is an atheist. I was raised with the belief that the only truth that matters is hard work. On the other hand, *Biji* was a devout Hindu. She believed in various ancient rituals and customs. One of those rituals was tying a *mauli* around my wrist while blessing me. I feel the threads don't protect you by themselves, but the energies and memories attached to them do. But after meeting His Holiness twice in two days, I knew some sort of energy was at play.'

That day onwards, Chef's belief in his own self got a boost, and his faith in himself was reignited. He began working on the planning of his future projects. Whether they were books, dishes, or documentaries; they were all his expressions to represent India to the world, in all her vibrant colours.

It only made him seek out more knowledge about various religious and spiritual realms of the world, which eventually took the form of a documentary, *Kitchens of Gratitude*, a summation of his travels and research spread across the years.

When the documentary released on 14 of May 2016, at the Cannes Film Festival, Chef's words rang in the hearts and minds of the people across religious and spiritual beliefs.

'I feel the power of faith in food; every morsel of food hides a universe inside it and brings it together. Whether it was during the time when I had meals at the homeless shelter, or while I was researching for my documentary, *Kitchens of Gratitude*, in Pakistan where the Harappa Civilisation used to thrive; and even in the places of worship of various religions across the world. I noticed there was one thing common—the sharing of food and bonding over it.'

When Chef had met His Holiness at the Waldorf Astoria, His Holiness had told him that 'bigger things are coming your way'. All it took was a little faith.

'PEACE' OF BREAD

Each one of us has a potential to make a better world.
—His Holiness the Dalai Lama

It was the start of the bitter winters in northern India in 1990 when twenty-four chairs, twenty-four plates, and three big pots made their way to the Khanna abode in Amritsar.

In the past few days, a small space in the back of their house had been the centre of hectic activity, as it saw the people to whom it had been rented out, move on to a new chapter in their lives. Soon after everyone was gone, the empty space gave rise to many ideas in Chef's mind. He wanted to use it for a small banquet.

'At that time, I didn't even know what a restaurant was. I had seen my mom go for these kitty parties and I knew food could be arranged for such parties.'

The family was hesitant about giving up the rent that was small but still invaluable in its contribution to the family's overall income. But Chef, who was only eighteen at that time, had gained confidence in his cooking skills by catering for a wedding only a few days ago. He was not going to back down and had already begun trying to figure out a plan to arrange the all important start-up capital.

'First, I worked at the Amritsar Club and helped them out by buying glassware on their behalf at a price that was very cheap. In the process, I made INR 400, which was less than USD 25 at that time.'

But that was not enough. He knew he had to take his efforts to the next level and take up a challenging job he knew about. Chef and his mother found out that Vivek Public School at the Mall Road was in need of handmade sweaters for its students, and he had even managed to convince Mrs Bawa, the Principal, to give them the job. It sounded like a good plan to begin with, but there was one hitch. Chef had no experience in knitting.

Once again, his family showed faith in his abilities and he went to *Biji* who taught him how to knit, while his mother helped him buy the wool and a knitting machine he needed, on credit. The journey was not easy. Even after burning the midnight oil each day after school, when he managed to take some samples to the school, Mrs Bawa, upon looking at the tiny necks of the sweaters, had to remind him that the woollens had to be worn by actual students.

Maybe the stars were in his favour because Mrs Bawa gave him some more time. Under the watchful eyes of *Biji* and his mother, they managed to deliver 580 blue sweaters in time before the grey winters of 1990 took over the streets of Amritsar. They earned the money that was needed to start the business—INR 15,000, which was about USD 900 in those days.

But at the time when all the hectic activities were underway in the family, he was not the only one who was knitting. His father, too, had knitted up a surprise for him. Soon after the order had been completed, on Chef's nineteenth birthday, his father presented him with a small tandoor that cost INR 250 or about USD 15 at that time, to help him start the business. At the heart of every catering business that serves Punjabi cuisine lies a tandoor which is used to cook the breads, kebabs and the famous *tandoori chicken*. But this tandoor, painted blue on the outside, was too small to be able to sustain the demand that Chef was hoping for the business to have. It made him so upset that he did not even thank his father for the gift.

But he soon made peace with the size of the tandoor, because it was something he had wanted for a long time. His friends wanted books, televisions, bicycles, video games and cricket bats to play with, but not him. Whenever he could sneak out of his home after school, he didn't go to the playground. Instead, he went and practised making breads and kebabs in a small shop at Maqbool Road near his home.

And when he finally got the gift he wanted, he spent the entire day at his favourite hang-out, where he learnt the practical aspects of operating the tandoor: how to start and control the fire and the temperature inside, the places where the breads and kebabs could be put, and how to clean it. Even today, when he visits Amritsar and goes to that shop where it all started, a little smile lights up his face.

After learning the art of using the tandoor, *Biji* helped him perform the sacred ceremony of rubbing it with a little bit of brine before lighting the fire. And just as he was about to place the first piece of bread inside it, she asked him to break a tiny piece of dough, almost as small as the edge of his thumb and offer it to the fire, because she believed, 'You should offer the first morsel to the fire that feeds you.' He asked her why, and she said that the ritual was close to her heart because, 'Every time we light a fire, the charcoal burns itself to help us make our food. The small piece of bread is a mark of respect for its sacrifice.' The words struck a chord with him. Even today when he stokes a fire in any new kitchen, he offers the first morsel to it.

'We were never a family that had any food business, but we decided to go ahead with that experiment of our lives to express our love for food. That is how the Lawrence Garden Catering Company was born on 2 December 1990.'

The reason why that particular date was chosen is also very interesting.

'2 December that year was a Sunday, and Mrs Bawa was not available on any other day because she had to be at the school. Since she was the guest of honour, we moved the date to suit her schedule.'

But as Lawrence Garden was coming into existence that morning and the equipment was making its way towards it, even before the business could actually start, one of the plates broke. The number of plates and chairs, and the resultant capacity of the business were already limited by the small capital they had invested. Help came in the form of two orange sofas that were loaned by Chef's mother's childhood friend, Rani Aunty, who took the two pieces of furniture right out of her home to fuel the young businessman's aspirations. But soon they found that even that was not enough.

Following a passion is one thing, but turning it into a reality, especially a business, an entirely different proposition. Chef realised this as he and his mother began running the business. During the first six months, each time they had an event, if the number of guests exceeded their capacity, they had to take things on rent. The staff, the cookware and plates, the tables, everything was hired in such scenarios. Since they did not have a refrigerator, all the excess food was distributed among the staff. Also, since the kitchen was out in the open, Chef had a constant fear that it would rain right before the event and all the food that they had prepared would get spoilt. Sadly, sometimes, it did.

'I still have a recurring dream; I'm sitting in Lawrence Garden, cooking in the kitchen without a roof, in the middle of a dark, overcast day, and it is about to rain.'

All of that affected the profits.

But thankfully, the hard work eventually paid off as they were able to secure a few steady catering assignments which helped them turn the tide. They were able to buy their own equipment, and slowly, word spread across the city which helped them to sustain the business.

There was something about the blue colour of the sweaters, and that of the blue tandoor, that gives Chef hope each time he sees it till today. He might not have thanked his father that day for the gift, but the seeds of 'peace' had been sown in that blue tandoor.

'At that time I knew what I was doing was not a viable business. It was more of a series of social events my mother and I used to host, while *Biji* cooked in the background, but we continued doing it out of love. We had to cut my favourite lime and mango trees in the garden that housed the business to make space, but I knew that this garden we had created with our hard work was helping us make the lives of the people of Amritsar a tad happier. It was one of the best things that came out of running Lawrence Garden.

'*Biji* used to tell us that the bigger the pots and pans, the bigger was the heart of the kitchen. She felt that if someone asked for a second helping, it meant that they had liked the food and, for her, it was the only way one could express love. My father used to say that *Biji* and I should have changed the name of our business to "Lawrence Garden Charity", but *Biji* believed everything was like a boomerang.

Everything came back. "You feed their kids—and their kids will come and feed you. Nothing disappears.'"

But when Chef went to America, he missed *Biji*'s constant presence and words of advice. And that vacuum only grew after her passing. The distance between Chef and his first mentor was now not limited to only a few thousand miles and that is something that Chef was reminded of every day when he saw the *mauli* that she had given to him. But it also brought a sense of revelation.

'*Biji* may not be there with me today, but every time I serve someone a "peace" of bread, she is present as my guardian angel.'

THE NIGHT I ALMOST DIED

You've to die a few times before you can really live.
—Charles Bukowski

A comet is a spectacle in the night skies; it burns, bright as the day, capturing the imagination of many, young and old alike. But while it is beautiful, it also burns itself to give light to the cosmos.

After landing in America in early December 2000, Chef began the struggles in the pursuit of his dream—the dream of becoming a Michelin-starred chef. Jobs were easy to come by because, in New York, everyone has a tendency to move fast. All he had to do was meet the owners of the restaurants, and begin working in the position that was vacant. He knew that a moving wheel gathers no moss, and he kept trying to get a job in an establishment that would allow him to cook and serve food. Eventually, his persistence was rewarded as he got a job in a small deli.

'Over the years, I've figured out something that has become a thumb rule for me. You only give names to things and people significant to you. There are millions of pigeons around here, but till the pigeon is yours you will not name it. And that is why I'm not going to give a name to the deli or the chef there. I'm going to call him Chef XYZ. But he taught me an important lesson too,' said Chef.

Chef XYZ did not like Chef at all. And one day, when he told the dishwasher about his dream of getting a Michelin star, Chef XYZ's hatred only increased.

'I looked away as he tried to find ways to provoke me, and focused only on the work assigned to me. He kept telling me to go back to India and that I would not amount to anything in New York. But I knew I only wanted to learn and acquire some gold dust from the vast treasure chests of food knowledge that New York City and its immigrants have. And then things got really bad. I remember it was well past midnight and the dinner service had ended an hour ago. Everyone had left, except me, as usual. I was given the additional task of ensuring that the kitchen was clean and ready for the breakfast service the next day. And after I had finished, the chef wanted me to clean the freezer with hot water because he claimed that we did not keep it clean. I knew something was fishy, but I also knew that I could not say no. So, I entered the freezer and, right after, I heard a click behind me.'

Chef was locked inside and there was no way he could come out on his own. There was no one who could open the door from outside because Chef XYZ had ensured all the staff members had left for the night.

One cannot spend a night in a commercial freezer; beyond a few minutes, panic hits and one can lose consciousness due to the lack of oxygen. And eventually, death swoops in quietly.

Even today, thinking about this 'frigid' memory leads to a chill running up Chef's spine.

'I kept knocking from inside, but I knew everyone had left for the day. Normally, the chef used to leave as soon as the owners had left for their homes, but that night he stuck around. Some days he used to tell me he would burn my face with hot oil and some days he threatened to chop my fingers off, slamming a cleaver on the chopping board while I was at work. I thought about why I had not responded to those threats. Why had I not said no when he asked me to clean the freezer after everyone else had left?'

But then, there was another hand at play that night; the hand of Karma. The good wishes of all those who he had helped in his life intervened.

'The dishwasher was waiting near the back door of the deli. Soon after Chef XYZ left, he snuck back into the restaurant and opened the door of the freezer. But he had no idea he would find me in there. He had only come to steal ice cream. When he saw me, he thought that I too was trying to steal something.'

The next day, when Chef got to work, after the breakfast service, he took a break saying he had to go to the bank and he started looking for other jobs. He knew that the person who had threatened him many times and tried to kill him once might try again. And he might achieve what he wanted.

When he found a job at another deli a few weeks after quitting working for Chef XYZ, a few days before Christmas in 2000, they forgot to inform him they were closed, and he found himself on the streets of New York, broke, with no steady job, cold and scared. That was the time when he was forced to live in the New York Rescue Mission.

In the midst of the freezing winters, Chef decided to resort to the rescue mission for a few days because he felt safe there. And he managed to find a silver lining to those times. He learnt how to cook Cajun-spiced chicken to perfection and managed to win hearts of everyone there with his food. He realised he already had experience in catering and should try his luck at doing something of his own. A chance came his way as he got a catering order to cook 300 portions of appetisers for a party on a yacht. Catering was something he had done back home and the first order paved the way for a steady stream of catering assignments. He supplemented the income from these assignments by cooking Indian food at the homes of the Indians who had started coming to America to work as the IT industry boomed. He even did household chores for the people he was cooking for to further augment his income, while he continued his search for a job that would allow him the creative freedom to be able to do what he wanted without any encumbrances. Eventually, he got a job at a restaurant called *Salaam Bombay*, where he started by doing odd jobs. The times were difficult post the 9/11 attacks in New York City, and there was scepticism in the air. But slowly he began getting more responsibilities as he got the opportunity of managing the restaurant and took steps towards understanding the way restaurants run in America. That also led to him getting a chance to show his creativity by crafting special menus and even cooking special meals. But his creative hunger kept looking for more.

Chef remembers that during those trying times, the words of one of his favourite poems, 'Still I Rise', by Maya Angelou, kept him going:

> *You may write me down in history*
> *With your bitter, twisted lies,*
> *You may tread me in the very dirt*
> *But still, like dust, I'll rise.*

Such was the impact of the poem, combined with his belief that the only way one can overcome a fear was by facing it, that he continued looking for better opportunities without being scared. His learning at *Salaam Bombay* helped him run things at *Tandoor Palace*, the restaurant where he worked next. It was here where he was put in charge of the kitchen along with the managing of the entire restaurant. Slowly, his passion for food began to be noticed by various patrons of this new workplace, and then life changed like never before when fate, in the form of Gordon Ramsay, chose him to be a part of a show on television.

When the dark clouds in his life had given way to golden rays of sunshine, Chef even enrolled for flying lessons to overcome yet another fear! He attended classes in Long Island by managing to squeeze in some time. Even though he wasn't able to finish the course, given his busy schedule, he achieved what he had set out to—he overcame his fear of heights.

At times, we face immense, unforeseen hardships, but to quote the German philosopher Friedrich Nietzsche, 'What doesn't kill you makes you stronger.'

And when he began to hear things like, 'The only reason why I'm here in Manipal today is you,' that a new student of WGSHA said to him during a Skype call with the new batch of 2016, during their induction ceremony on 30 July 2016, all the struggles became worth the pain.

THE COLOUR OF ALL

A dream you dream alone is only a dream. A dream you dream together is reality.
—John Lennon

Different people have different traits. Whether it is the members of a family, or the players in a football team, and even the kitchen's staff—some bring red, bright energy; others, golden troves of experience; then there are those gems with white innocence and yet others with silvery, steely determination; the colours of 'all' teach different things at different points in life.

Once it was a holiday, but Chef, who was still a young teenager studying in school, was nowhere to be found. As there were no cell phones in those times, it had led to a panic in the house. But then the frantic searching came to an unexpected halt as a little while later his mother found him walking into the house with some plants in his hands with his *bua* in tow. Ninni *Bua*, or the Little Aunt, as he used to call her fondly, and Chef had taken off to buy some plants from Beas, a small town that is a short drive away from Amritsar.

Chef has always had a soft corner for plants and animals because many memories of time spent with the family are attached to them.

There was a mango tree in their backyard he loved, because each summer, it gave the family fresh mangoes. And mangoes meant mango ice cream. The family had an old ice cream machine that used to be worked with a crank. It took a long time, which was why *Biji* made all of the children sit in a circle around the machine and take turns to crank it. Sometimes, she made them wait longer than needed. The wait and the aching arms were often made fun of by Chef's younger sister, Radhika. The mango tree was witness to the laughter and anticipation that echoed through the house. And when the ice cream was finally ready, it used to watch them relish the fruits of their labour, smiling with contentment.

But then time changed gears and brought along a present—an electric ice cream machine.

'As soon as *Biji* saw it, she rejected it. We didn't know at that time, but she knew it would be the "end of ice cream" for us in the way we had known it through our childhood. There was no need for us to sit and take turns to churn the mix, no aching arms and no jokes. The fun was gone from the entire process.

The old machine was used only a couple of times and then forgotten along with the laughter and anticipation.

'Einstein had once said that "everything should be made as simple as possible, but not simpler." That day, I learned something *Biji* had always known. Technology makes our job easier in some ways, but it can also take away the small, unexpected joys that come along with old-fashioned work.'

Another plant that evokes memories for Chef is the humble potato. They did not have a kitchen garden in their home in Amritsar, but there was a time, during the year of the Punjab Emergency, when they had nothing except a bag of potatoes to feed an entire family.

In 1984, when Operation Blue Star was on, a state of Emergency was imposed in Punjab. Amritsar was at the heart of the conflict, and the city was cordoned off to aid the army operations, which resulted in no electricity for many weeks. Even the food and water supplies from other parts of the country were cut off, which led to a serious shortage in the city. Somehow, the family managed to get hold of a large sack of potatoes and that was all that they had to feed themselves for many days. Each day, the same potato curry was served for every meal.

And one day, Chef, who was a young boy of thirteen, refused to eat more of the same potato curry. He was sick of the same food. People around them were starving, but his young mind did not realise the gravity of the situation that the city was facing. On seeing this, *Biji* smiled and said, 'Viku, this is not potato curry. It is curry potato.'

He smiled and ate the curry potato.

As the years passed, *Biji's* smile and the lesson without words inspired him.

'Even in those dire times, *Biji* taught me that food was a blessing. There was not much to feed us, but whatever we had was used with love. Today, I'm full of gratitude for each morsel I am fortunate enough to have. I may be able to make and eat the most expensive food in the world, but it would not mean much if I could not share it with the people around me.'

A few years later, when Chef was in his college in Manipal studying hotel management, Professor YG Tharakan took him under his wings seeing his hunger to learn during the interview for the admission. While he was a tough taskmaster and a strict disciplinarian, he also taught his students the value of the colour of 'all'.

Professor Tharakan knew each of the students of Chef's batch by their first name. Theirs was one of the first batches in the college and the small number of students made that possible. He even knew the parents of his students well enough to be able to ensure that each of them progressed well. As the years passed, many of those people ceased to be just parents of his students and became friends. And such were those bonds that even after all these years he is friends with many of them.

Chef continues to adhere to the lessons from Manipal and his mentor wherever he goes.

The tradition of being aware of the surroundings and taking part in the lives of his staff, friends and family continues to this very day. Whenever there is a birthday of a staff member of the restaurant, it is celebrated together with as many other staff members as possible, which includes Chef too, if he is not travelling.

At times when any member of his staff makes him proud by winning accolades in competitions across the world, they have a devout cheerleader in him. So, whether it was when Aarthi Sampath, the Indian Chef—an integral part of Chef's kitchens and books—became the first Indian woman chef to win the American reality-based cooking show, *Chopped*, or when his college mates from WGSHA were winning rave reviews and accolades across the world—they always had Chef standing in the corner like a silent guardian.

Another important lesson that he got to learn during his days in Manipal was that in the local cuisine.

Professor Tharakan recalls that 'Vikas learned the local cuisine from the members of the staff of the college who hailed from nearby areas. He even used to go to their homes to learn the intricacies of delicate flavours that were very different from the ones he had grown up with in northern India. He would finish the work that was assigned to him first, and then continue working afterwards to hone his knowledge about the diverse flavours in Manipal and the surrounding areas.'

Chef also bought various cookbooks and food magazines from the local scrap market. He got them cheap, but the lessons he learnt from them were invaluable. And later, as he gained confidence about the local cuisine, reading those magazines along with the coursebooks, he began to experiment with the food and its plating.

'Each time I hear the word "twist", I'm reminded of Vikas. While I taught the students presentation and insisted on sticking to the book, whenever possible, he would twist things. I let him do that because he would first do the presentation in the authentic way I had taught him and then use his creativity,' says the Professor.

Today Chef tells his staff to abide by the rule book. And if they want freedom to express their creativity, it comes at a price.

But everything comes at a price. In Chef's kitchens, freedom is given to those who earn it with their hard work and persistence. He always tells his staff what his mother used to tell him: 'Follow your heart and be like a sponge, because it may take many years for you to own your own kitchen, but till then learn as much as you can. And when the time comes, own it, literally and figuratively, since it takes a lot to earn it.'

'Yet another lesson I learned from my mom was that of persistence, no matter what. While hosting the kitty parties at Lawrence Garden, she stood and watched over everything even if the parties continued for hours. Each and every guest was greeted with the same, welcoming smile,' says Chef.

Chef has followed this lesson from his boyhood days everywhere, whether it is in the kitchens of his restaurants or on the sets of his television shows, he never says no to anyone when they approach him for help.

Celebrated Indian restaurateur, Zorawar Kalra, was a judge with Chef in the fifth season of *MasterChef India*. He had a rather interesting observation about Chef.

'He is cut from a different cloth,' Zorawar observed as he saw Chef treat the members of the staff on the sets, his fellow judges and any other person who visited the set, with the same warmth and love, even when it was towards the end of a day filled with the rigours of a long, tiring shoot.

And sometimes when he is in a different time zone, talking to the students of his alma mater, even if it is well past midnight, he takes questions from each and every starry-eyed student and nurtures their dreams.

'Everyone has their own individual colour and that is what makes the palette complete. I feel that singular societies don't work anymore. Sometimes when you get knocked down by life, there is no need for words because all that is needed is a silent, loving hug.'

Life is a tough teacher; it gives the test first, and the lesson later. The initial days in America that saw Chef struggle for survival while he did so many odd jobs that he lost count, might have been the phase when this teacher taught him some invaluable lessons—the silent, dark pain of sleeping on an empty stomach; the bitter, bone-chilling pain of not having a roof over one's head; and the lesson of valuing the real wealth—the beauty of the colour of 'ALL', the people.

BARAKA

Honesty and transparency make you vulnerable.
Be honest and transparent anyway.
—Saint Teresa of Calcutta

'Baraka' is a blessing recited during religious ceremonies. It is more than a word—an emotion and a whole lot of faith for Chef.

There was a member in Chef's maternal family—a wisened, grey-haired man with a warm smile. The man was not related to them by blood, but he was the one whose food had nourished the young and the old in the family for fifty years. Since his boyhood, each time Chef visited his maternal home in Amritsar, he would touch the feet of his elders, including the smiling old man, Dhaniram. His name means someone who is wealthy, and for Chef, Dhaniram was one of the wealthiest men, one who got blessings from the entire family after he had fed them food.

These seeds of wealth that were sown right from Chef's childhood are what make him seek the blessings of his elders and his mentors each time he meets them. During the shooting of one his shows, *Twist of Taste*, he visited Manipal to relive the days when he used to study there. And when he met his mentor, Professor YG Tharakan, he touched his feet.

'Whatever I am today is because of Tharakan Sir,' Chef proclaimed on national television.

Success is a wheel made up of a lot of spokes. Every wheel is unique. But if there is one common thread that ties them together, it is humility.

'Many people think chefs have a quick temper and are difficult to work with. While it is true that tempers do fly sometimes when there is pressure to deliver hot, perfect, pre-plated meals to a room packed with people, it is an exception, not the norm. I've been fortunate to have got the opportunity to work with Chef Gordon Ramsay on multiple occasions and, each time, I've observed his warmth towards the entire team. The people, too, reciprocate it by showing loyalty towards him that goes well beyond their professional duties.'

And that is what Chef also tries to emulate in his life as much as possible.

Jason DiTullio, one of Chef's closest friends and confidantes, remembers the time when they met for the first time while he was working in *Salaam Bombay* in 2001.

'He was not the fearless, funny New Yorker he is today, because he had just moved to America. But everything else about him is the same even today. He has not let the madness around him get to him and, even today, he treats everyone the same, whether it is a CEO dining with him, or the staff of the set's canteen which serves the crew food.'

But sometimes Chef has been dishonest too.

During the era of handmade trousers and radios, Chef was a young boy who had just turned twelve. On his birthday, his mother got him a piece of cloth so that they could get it stitched into new trousers for him. The piece of cloth was stored in a metal almirah so that it could be taken to the tailor the next day. But his young mind had other plans. He lied to his mother that he was going out to play. Chef got on his tiny, old bicycle and went to the shop where she had bought the cloth to return it, and with that money he bought a transistor for her. The black, pink and blue radio in their family home in Amritsar might be obsolete today, but for his mother it is worth its weight in gold.

'Mom owns very few clothes and even fewer for special occasions. She only worries about her children, friends, the members of our entire extended family and even the neighbours. The person at the end of that list is her own self. And like her, brands and materialistic things hold very little space in Viku's mind and heart,' Radhika shares.

Radhika is a fashion designer based in New York, and tries to give him fashion advice, but more often than not, most of it falls on deaf ears. He is focused on things he feels are more important. Whether it is the homecoming of *Utsav* at the place he worships—WGSHA, or when he is hosting a charity dinner for the Smile Foundation, the organisation that is his partner in all the work he does for nutrition of underprivileged children in India; and even during the launch of his documentary, *Kitchens of Gratitude,* amid the glitterati on the red carpet at Cannes, his focus is on the task at hand and not on how he is looking. He owns only a few black T-shirts and a few pairs of jeans. Most of the clothes he wears at these events are generally given away to the staff at the venues, and sometimes returned. Even gifts like clothing, shoes, chocolate and bags find their way to friends and other people around him. This leads to problems too: problems such as not having the right clothes to wear to certain events, much to the chagrin of the people organising them. But then solutions are found then and there—like borrowing pants from his brother, Nishant; a coat from a friend, and rummaging through his bags to find a right pair of socks to walk in on the red carpet.

And for Chef, 'Life goes on. No one will die if I don't wear matching socks at an event.'

But then, there are a few items Chef owns and takes pride in—his treasure trove of chef coats collected over the years, and an enviable collection of the best chef knives from across the world—each one of them a little piece of magic that has helped him preserve the memories and aromas associated with the times when he used them.

When he is travelling, he prefers to stay in hotels because, 'It takes away the tension of having to worry about cleaning, laundry and other such things during the schedules when I don't even have time to sleep.'

The only exceptions to this are the times he visits his mother in Amritsar or his brother and his nieces in Delhi. There, his mother and his sister-in-law, Shelly Khanna, spoil him with sumptuous meals. These are the times when the man who cooks for the world gets to eat food made by those who mean the world to him. And in these moments, the dieting and weight-watching disappears.

Fun moments like these are what matter more to him than other things like clothes and appearances. And sometimes, these small nuggets are hidden away in the middle of a mall at the end of a busy day.

Once Chef stopped at a mall near the sets of *MasterChef India* to buy a pair of socks. But when the salesperson told him that the shop only had a pack of three pairs and not a single pair, Chef told him that he needed just one and argued about how the other two pairs would never be used. It wasn't about the cost of the socks, but about finding joy in the banter.

Kapil Motwani was a part of the team from Star TV taking care of the shooting of *MasterChef India* when Chef made his first appearance on Indian television. It was a tense season for Chef as the show was going to be watched by millions, and this time it was not in America but his motherland, India. But Kapil remembers, 'Despite all the stress, Vikas never shied away from interacting with everyone on the sets. He posed for selfies whenever anyone requested them, ate with the crew in the same dining area and even cracked jokes whenever he saw that things were getting tense. He is a quintessential tension-breaker and does it effortlessly by doing simple things like making fun of his own accent, or the dressy clothes that he would be asked to wear during the shoots of special episodes. And this trait of his has ripples that last well beyond the time he spends with the people around him.'

One such ripple was felt by a lady named Rupa Shah. Shah was a part of the audience that watches *MasterChef India*, and over time, as she watched the episodes of the show, her desire to meet Chef became a reason that gave her motivation to fight a monster we know as breast cancer.

'Rupa Ji, you're absolutely right; people who don't believe in magic will never find it,' Chef whispered when they got to meet and exchange stories.

Miracles happen every day and everywhere. It is for us to notice them and maybe even make them happen. And not letting failures keep us down is one such miracle.

Maybe these incidents that have been 'occurring' in Chef's life right from his boyhood have been laying foundations for the 'buildings' that he has built in his life. After all, good Karma echoes through the universe. Maybe Baraka leads the way wherever we go.

4:30 AM

If the creative artist worries if he will still be free tomorrow,
then he will not be free today.
—Salman Rushdie

Magic: five letters that evoke a million thoughts in the
mind. Each heart imagines it in a different way. The
shining sparkles, the peals of laughter and sometimes, even
the tears of joy; magic is hidden in many hues.

And just like magic, magicians too are of different kinds.
Some wave, others weave and a few paint. And many of them
share a common love—a love for the dark, twinkling magic
of the night.

This is the time when the singer forgets everything around
her, lost in her world behind closed eyes; she forgets even
herself as she listens to her soul singing. Somewhere in those
moments of silence, the poet hears his own self—the self that

is drowned by the sounds of the world during the day and then the ink bleeds. And it is sometime during these hours that the designs of the universe come to fore in the heart of the artist and take worldly forms amid a riot of talking colours.

'Silence is one of the biggest motivations for creativity. And the most creative hour of the day for me is from 4:30 to 5:30 am,' Chef shares.

'I realised this during my travels through the Himalayas. The monks there wake up at the crack of dawn, sometimes even earlier and spend the hours before the world wakes up, immersed in meditation. I feel some sort of a connection with the mountains. The more I travel there, the more I feel centred and rejuvenated. I grow and yet I am the same. And now, whenever I'm suffering from a creative block, I try to think about the monks' peaceful faces. I think about how their food keeps evolving though the traditions remain the same. It is all like a perfect mandala, the perfectly balanced symbol that represents wisdom and compassion in the Buddhist religion. The centre of the wheel remains fixed, while we revolve around it.'

For Chef, the word synonymous with a perfect mandala is 'kitchen'.

The kitchen in the home where Chef was born and raised was one of the parts of the house where he spent the maximum time. In his early years, it was his safe haven away from all the jibes of the world about his misaligned feet. It was where his little heart fell in love with the world of food. And such was the love that later in his life, when all the other children his age played various sports in the playgrounds, he was in the kitchen playing with pots and pans.

'The damp walls, yellow paint peeling off in patches, and the yellow door that looked like it had been painted with turmeric—these are the images that come to my mind whenever I think of kitchens because that is how the kitchen in my home in Amritsar used to look. In that kitchen, there was a single window right above the cooking range. In those times, the holy fires in the kitchens used to be fuelled by charcoal. That had led to the window being covered with soot. It looked like a blemish on the wall, but in the night when there was no electricity due to the power cuts in the city, the window let in the moonlight to light up the kitchen. And sometimes when I sat there in the kitchen bathed in moonlight, some lines from the poems that *Bauji* read to us would come back to me,' Chef remembers.

This love for poetry that he inherited from his *Bauji* blossomed over the years in the form of words in his books such as *Utsav*, his culinary epic on Indian festivals; *Flavors First*, his book about Indian flavours and traditions in America; and even *Poeatry*, a book on poetry that he is penning.

Inspiration often strikes in the most unexpected places and times—sometimes while you're standing on one leg in a yoga pose, holding your breath, and sometimes when you're curled up in a warm blanket that feels just right and sleep is right around the corner, or even in the middle of tears. Whenever the words knock on Chef's door, he is ready.

But according to Chef, one extremely important factor for inspiration to hit home is lack of noise.

'In my childhood, I had the shade of the mango tree in my backyard and the long walks with *Bauji* when we went to get vanilla ice cream, coupled with conversations about poems.'

But now, he often writes poems and books in the lap of fluffy, white clouds, flying across the globe.

'There is no connectivity, no constant ringing and beeping of the phone, no noise.'

Whenever he wants inspiration on a flight, he switches to something that is both an inspiration and a stress buster, as well a source of pure joy—music.

Back in Amritsar, in his boyhood days, Chef used to listen to a song he felt was hypnotic and soothing. But in those times, there was no internet, or YouTube or Shazam; the music played from the little stereo as it read the magnetic tape, and got imprinted on Chef's mind.

'Life has a funny way of bringing things full circle. In the summer of 2001, when I enrolled for a course in the Culinary Institute of America, the CIA, I had a roommate who started playing music in our room. He saw me staring at the stereo with a blank expression on my face and asked if I was being disturbed. I was too transfixed to react. It was only a few moments later that I told him that the song he was playing was one of my favourite songs, but I had no idea who the singer was. After a little while, when the entire album had ended, I saw the cover and came to know the name of the singers for the first time—Simon and Garfunkel.'

The music of the duo had inspired Chef for all these years. It had even spurred the painter in him. He had begun to train under Gangadhar Sir, a renowned artist who lives in Udupi, a small town near Manipal.

And that day, he finally got to know their names.

Names are very important. They give an identity to people and things, and these little combinations of alphabets even have the power of spurring the imaginations of people many years after the passing of the ones who had those names. One name that inspires Chef is that of the master, Michelangelo.

During his initial days in America, when he was a regular at the library on the 42nd Street and 5th Avenue, he came in touch with inspiration in the form of a book about Michelangelo and the Sistine Chapel. Ever since he had seen the images of the chapel for the first time, he knew he had to see it in person. The opportunity came in the summer of 2010.

'Each stroke of the Sistine Chapel is so exquisitely well defined that one can almost see what Michelangelo was thinking when he painted it, hanging from the ceiling for hours every day. All of us have a Sistine Chapel buried deep inside us. One may find it in the way a little piece of bread rises up beautifully or in the way the milk rises above when the heat threatens to burn it, or even in the way a little child's face lights up when he makes his perfectly round chapati. It is for us to find the inspiration, lie on our backs and paint our Sistine Chapels.'

THE BALANCE OF BREAKS

Don't underestimate the value of doing nothing, of just going
along, listening to all the things you can't hear,
and not bothering.
—Winnie the Pooh

It was like any other day for most of the people in Gurugram, a satellite city in northern India that is a part of the National Capital Region. Most people were trying to get back from their offices and were stuck in the midst of blaring horns and the evening traffic.

But there was a different problem inside a small shop in a mall next to the crowded road. Chef, clad in black T-shirt and a pair of jeans was hiding under a blue beret, as he tried to pick the best fish from the lot being sold, without attracting much attention because he was in Gurugram only for a couple of days and he wanted to spend as much time as possible with his nieces, Saumya and Ojasvi.

'When I had asked Saumya what she wanted to eat that night for dinner, she had told me she wanted fish, and her wish is my command. Cooking with and for my nieces is something I look forward to. And whenever I'm in India, I ensure that I make time to spend a few days with them. We cook, bake, crack jokes and even watch television. They're the biggest supporters of my shows as well as the harshest critics. And sometimes when I ask them if they want to learn to cook Indian desserts, they laugh and frown and eventually we end up baking something French or American. But I'm fine with that, because they're still learning. I always try to encourage them to learn something new every day.'

This was something that was imbibed in Chef by *Biji* in his childhood while he was learning to cook, knit, make ice cream or do anything that caught his fancy. *Biji* always encouraged him to learn something new and the naughty glint in his eyes used to make her heart melt in an instant.

Jude Sir, who used to teach Mathematics to Chef in school, still remembers Chef's smile, 'Vikas's smile hasn't changed since he was a little boy. I see him whenever he is in Amritsar and comes to visit me despite his incredibly busy schedule, but even if he isn't here in town, when I hear Vikas's name, I think about the naughty glint in his eyes as he smiles.'

As a child, Chef was lost in his own world and was seldom caught in situations where he needed to use his smile to get out of them.

'Radhika has always been into travelling. She has seen almost every nook and corner of the world now, but I remember the time when it all started. She told me she wanted to go to Bangkok with me, but she did not want to tell anyone at home about it, because if we did, they would never let us go. So, we left home telling the family that we were going to visit our relatives in Delhi and ended up in Bangkok. When we ran out of money, we started fighting and had to call our elder brother, Nishant, to be rescued. He too did not send us money; he came down to Bangkok to be with us. But it was only when he arrived that we realised that before anything else, we were going to have to face him and the anger of the entire family.'

But Chef's smile smoothened everything out in a matter of a few hours, and Nishant ended up becoming the official photographer for the duo on the trip.

And many years later, when Chef moved to America, Radhika continued to be his partner-in-crime.

'Chef David Waltuck used to run *Chanterelle*, which was one of the most iconic food destinations across the world. It broke my heart when it shut down in 2009 after being a paradise I looked forward to for many years. I still remember I used to pass it while I was working at *Salaam Bombay*; each time I saw it, I would dream of eating there someday.'

But when Chef managed to save enough to be able to go there for a meal, he did not go. He continued to save and only when he had enough to take his sister along, he took her there without even telling her where they were going. He feels that good food is one of the most exquisite as well as essential experiences that each and every one should have in their lives, whenever possible. It became a ritual for Chef and Radhika. Each time he saved up enough for the two of them, he would spend it on an expensive brunch at his favourite restaurants in New York City.

'When you're sitting on a beach, watching the sunset, or you get a phone call for which you've been waiting since the day you began working, or when you're eating that perfect peach in the morning for breakfast, some special people come to your mind. The ones you want to share these moments with, even if they are not there with you. They could be friends, family or someone else. I learned to cherish these moments from *Biji* somewhere during the endless hours of making ice cream with the hand-cranked machine with my siblings and friends. She used to tell us that if we didn't value those moments and those people, a day might come when we would look back at all the success and the medals and the wealth, but still feel as if we had nothing.'

And that also makes him break into impromptu singing and dancing bouts in the middle of events, sometimes at being egged on by others and sometimes all on his own, much to the delight of the others.

'Recreation is an important part of creativity,' he believes, and tries to include it in his daily routine, whether it is in the form of spending time with his mother, his nieces or other family members. Unplanned trips to the hinterlands of India just to know more about something, like a new technique of cooking someone has told him about and sometimes a walk on Brooklyn Bridge at the end of a strenuous day count as recreation.

The power of doing nothing is one of the most important forces that has to be balanced with the power of hard work and perseverance. Ever so often one derives inspiration in these moments of calm exteriors accompanied by creative fervour. Whether it is the ringing laughter of Professor Tharakan or the words of Bill Watterson, 'There's never enough time to do all the nothing you want'—all of it inspires Chef as he constantly strives to strike a balance between work and breaks.

Even today, Tharakan Sir gets calls from Chef and his batchmates in America in the middle of the night. The time difference doesn't matter when one wants to share happiness, right?

And it isn't just Chef and his batchmates; even Tharakan Sir enjoys these moments with his students and recalls small incidents as good as new in his memory.

Tharakan Sir was known to be a disciplinarian and a strict taskmaster among all his students. He used to set up tough tests on a regular basis to gauge the ability of his wards. One day, he demonstrated how to make a shrimp cocktail sauce as Chef, Pallav Baruah, one of his closest friends at WGSHA, and the other students watched. Pallav and Chef were partners for this task and they decided to have some fun. After the demonstration was done, Pallav managed to sneak out some sauce made by Sir and presented it to him for assessment. On tasting it, Tharakan Sir commented, 'The tanginess is a bit inadequate.' Both Pallav and Chef burst out laughing.

After all, who knows which of these moments filled with fun and laughter that took our breath away in the past might light the spark of inspiration within us in the future?

BROKEN PEARLS

Attitude is a little thing that makes a big difference.
—**Winston Churchill**

Every child is subjected to some jibes while growing up. But what if the jibes are directed at something that is beyond his control?

'I was never a fit child. I used to hate the Biology class in school because the skeleton had my name written on it. The kids used to ask me if I had forgotten to get the two drops of Polio vaccination in my childhood.'

But he had an ace up his sleeve—his family: a family that ate together, stayed together and fought all the jibes together. And there was one indulgence too that the family enjoyed together. Their penchant for fitness and wholesome home-cooked meals was balanced with a tall, freshly made glass of cold coffee.

Whether it was at the end of a breakfast of *poha* and fruits, or along with *rajma-chawal* for lunch, or after dinner at their favourite restaurant, freshly made cold coffee was always—and still is—relished by all the family members, including Chef.

Ironically, while Chef is a man whose hands have fed many beautiful Indian flavours to others, his love for food lies in simple things. Probably due to what was ingrained in him during childhood, nothing cheers him up more than home-cooked food. And sometimes, when he is sick, he likes a piping hot bowl of *khichri* and yoghurt to have his health restored.

Even while he is shooting, he ensures he eats bowls of different kinds of *dal* made every day in the makeshift kitchens. The *dal*, and the occasional home-cooked meals brought by friends and family keep him going during the endless hours of shooting. But one thing that is beyond his penchant for fitness and home-cooked meals is the cold coffee that helps him in fighting the stress.

This love for simple food was crucial even for his fitness regime he had adopted to attain shape.

'What I love about the gyms in America is that you can visit them at any time of the day and night.'

After months of toiling at the gym, coupled with strict monitoring of his diet, he reached a point where people who mattered began to notice his efforts. And they remember those moments fondly. One such person, Hiroko Kiiffner, the founder of the New York-based Lake Isle Press, recalls such a day.

'It all began in our small publishing office on the upper west side of Manhattan, one day in February 2011. My colleague, Jenn Sit, announced in her soft voice that the New York-based foodie website, *Eater*, was running a contest for "The hottest chef in New York" and she had nominated Vikas, complete with a photograph. At that time, Vikas was rather shy, and I wasn't convinced he would like the attention. Nevertheless, we were amazed as votes came rolling in by thousands, and before we knew it, Vikas was New York's Hottest Chef!'

Many people had strong reactions to Chef's competing for the award and some even tried to put him down saying they didn't want to see him and the curries of Indians in America. They wanted him to go back. But these people had forgotten one essential quality of group dynamics.

Whenever there is an underdog, everyone wants him or her to win. Whenever a bully tries to put the underdog down, everyone tries to root for him—some do it openly and some do it silently through truckloads of votes.

That was proved when he was featured in the '50 Sexiest Men Alive' list prepared by the *People Magazine* in 2011. And when he won the title of 'New York's Hottest Chef' yet again in 2012, it even prompted *Eater* to say on their website that 'maybe next year, he will sit the contest out to give a chance to some of the other contenders of New York!'

And it kept getting proven again and again. In October 2012, he was featured on the cover of *Men's Health* magazine and even managed to get some comments from Chef Gordon Ramsay on national television.

'I had only one motive in mind when I worked on having six-pack abs at that time. I wanted to tell people that I only ate Indian food and that I too could look like that. I wanted to bust the myth that Indian food was unhealthy and that all the Indian chefs could only look a certain way. But then it was not easy. When other people started asking me to do similar cover shoots for their magazines, I refused because I had got what I had set out to achieve and I didn't want to fall prey to a fad.'

'You're too good-looking to be a Chef,' Gordon had said on camera when Chef appeared on his show, *Kitchen Nightmares*, for the second time in 2008. It had embarrassed Chef, given the fact that he was generally shy, but maybe the polls that followed in the years after the show were an affirmation of Gordon's comments by the millions who had watched the show.

But that does not mean that the old adage, 'You need to look like a movie star to succeed,' is right.

'Vikas is one of the most disciplined people that I've ever worked with,' says Ruchi Shrivastava, one of the members of the team that produced *MasterChef India* in the first few seasons. 'There was a party to celebrate the wrapping up of the Season 2 and everyone was indulging themselves with the choicest of food and drinks. But I noticed that after meeting everyone and posing for countless selfies, Vikas sat down in a corner with a bowl of papaya.'

She feels that, 'If there is one thing that I admire the most about Vikas, it is his discipline.'

Jason DiTullio, one of Chef's closest friends in New York, is of the view that, 'his focus on work, and ability to move on from any injuries, whether it is in the mind or the body and even relationships, help him. He is not someone who is affected by something like that for too long.'

Discipline and focus are two things that helped him even in the times when he was down and out.

'In 2010, while we were setting up *Junoon*, a few weeks before it opened to the public, I slipped and landed on the gas range, on my back. And once you injure your back, it becomes vulnerable. I had injured the L5 and L6 vertebrae at the first fall and then I kept injuring the same place each time I tried to lift something heavy. The body heats up when one is working in the kitchen; the heat, the steam and the running around led to a lot of physical pain at the end of almost each shift. So, I started going to the Derek Jetter gym near *Junoon* to try and stretch my back under supervision of a trainer to help my body heal naturally. I wanted to avoid surgery, but eventually I had to go through it because the pain became too much to bear.'

Ironically, while Chef was bedridden, trying to recuperate from the surgery, he got the news that he had been featured in the '50 Sexiest Men Alive' list of the *People* magazine.

'I joked with my manager, who had brought me the news, and asked him if they wanted to photograph me in the state I was in. My back felt like it was made of cement. At that time, I told him that only one thing could make me feel better: eating *methi-aloo*, which is a typical Indian preparation of fenugreek leaves and potatoes, made by my *Biji*. In my childhood, whenever I was sick, *Biji* used to make it and my sickness would vanish. I know I could have made it for myself, but what I could not have brought into it was her love to use as seasoning. In a few weeks, my back did get much better but, even today, sometimes I get spasms and my back becomes quite stiff. I know I've abused my body and I still work fifteen or sixteen hours every day. But I know I have to do it because I know that guys like me, the common people, get opportunities to do something truly significant very rarely. And I want to make the most of them.'

And of late, *Biji's* blessings have started showing as his back has begun recovering, just like his teeth did when he was a boy.

Chef's grandfather often told everyone that his first set of teeth looked like pearls. But when the milk teeth gave way to a permanent set of teeth, they turned out to be misaligned, much to the dismay of his mother. She knew money was an issue in the family, but she also knew that Chef needed braces and that she would manage to get them for him, no matter what. So, she took Chef to a dentist who accepted instalments from his patients for their treatments.

The treatment, though extremely painful and ancient, seemed to work, but then one day when Chef returned home after school, his mother saw him bleeding from his mouth and noticed that the braces were loose. She took him to the doctor immediately on her moped. Chef rode pillion with a little piece of Bindu Ji's handkerchief stuffed in his mouth to reduce the bleeding.

By the time they reached the doctor's clinic, Bindu Ji was in a panic. She wanted the doctor to hurry up and fix Chef's teeth, to which he remarked, 'What is the big deal? It is not as if he is going to become a movie star.'

Little did he know what Bindu Ji's dreams for her son were.

NEW YORKER OF THE WEEK

Helping others is the way we help ourselves.
—Oprah Winfrey

After emerging as a shy, young hotel management graduate from Manipal's WGSHA in the summer of 1994, the path led him to a slew of internships which saw him train at some of the hallowed hotels in India like the Taj and Oberoi, and then came a job at the Mumbai property of the Leela group of hotels. But a few years into the job, he decided to answer an inner calling and returned to his hometown, Amritsar, to take over the reins of Lawrence Garden, the family's catering business, which he had started at the age of nineteen and left in the care of his family before going to Manipal.

He had yet another reason that only a few souls knew about. It was Tiddy.

'Tiddy was a Pomeranian I had had since I was fifteen years old. She was tiny, which was why we had named her Tiddy—a Punjabi word for "small". She taught me what unconditional love was, but when she left me, I decided to never keep a pet again because I could never make myself go through the pain of losing a friend ever again.'

But love finds a way. His love for animals channelised into caring for the stray dogs around Lawrence Garden after Tiddy passed away. Even before that, he used to feed the dogs around in Manipal. He loved them so much that it almost got him expelled from his hostel on one occasion.

'We had a strict rule about not allowing any animals in the premises of the hostel, but once I caught Vikas with a puppy in his dorm in the middle of the night. It had yelped as I was passing by. I knew Vikas loved dogs, but I had to tell him that it was either the puppy or both of them who would have to leave the hostel,' Professor Tharakan recalls.

In Amritsar too, incidents surrounding dogs are etched in his mother's mind. She remembers that 'one day, I received a call from an angry woman asking me rudely where Viku was. When I asked her what the matter was, she said that he was three hours late that day and their dog had not eaten food!'

She was perplexed, but then she understood what was going on because she had seen Chef take some packets out every day from Lawrence Garden.

Chef still thinks about those days whenever he sees a dog. He recalls that 'a few days ago, I saw a tiny, frail dog with thinning, brown fur, probably due to hunger. It was our neighbour's dog, but they were vegetarians. So I started taking some leftover chicken for that dog.'

Even in America, the spirit of giving was never ebbed by the challenges he had to face there. Maybe it was the time he spent in the shelters for the homeless while trying to escape from the biting cold, when his resolve to help people was strengthened, because soon after cooking at the James Beard House on 23 August 2004, Chef began trying to host fundraisers.

It started at the *Tribeca Rooftop* in New York when he managed to convince them to host a fundraiser. One of his closest friends, Jason DiTullio, a resident New Yorker with Italian roots, remembers: 'He led by example right from the first time he hosted an event at *Tribeca*. He has the guts to get in touch with the biggest names because he knows he isn't selling anything. He is only trying to make a difference and he is so sincere about the cause that these people often end up following his lead and give more than what they normally would.'

Jason noticed with awe how he went about these fundraisers. Chef would say, 'I just called them; what did we have to lose?'

That is why, slowly but steadily, he was able to make a noticeable and sustained change in the lives of others.

Aryln Blake, a celebrated author, who used to work with the James Beard Foundation, remembers how Chef started to make a difference in the lives of others even as his own life was going through a transformation.

'As I remember, all the while he was working and supporting himself. He started small with cooking lessons for deaf and blind children in New York City, and before long he was organising a charity, bringing dozens of chefs to prepare dinners at the world's greatest monuments like the Pyramids and the Taj Mahal, and raising funds to build access ramps for handicapped children at these monuments. And he has not stopped. What astonishes me is that to this day, despite his crazy schedules where he is barely able to make time for a few hours of sleep, he is working for and providing funds for meals for thousands of children in India.'

The frenzied energy, Arlyn remembers, started soon after Chef cooked at the James Beard House. While he was hosting fundraisers, he also took up an opportunity that came from next door, quite literally.

'After quitting my job at *Salaam Bombay* in August 2004, I rented a kitchen on the 23rd Street which would accommodate ten to twelve people at a time. I wanted to start something of my own and I knew I'd need all the space that I could get. Soon, I began teaching people to cook Indian food. I tried to use my network at New York University to spread the word about the classes. It was very difficult in those times because there was no social media, but what helped me a lot to spread the word about my "Sanskrit Culinary Arts" were the favourable reviews from the attendees. But one place where I did not realise the word was spreading was right next door.'

A teacher from Selis Manor, a rehabilitation centre for visually impaired people, which was right next door, came by to meet Chef one morning and told him how they had been taking in the aroma of the food and the culture that he had been cooking up during the two months since he had rented the new kitchen and it had left everyone enchanted. She felt that such enchanting food had the power to enhance the life of the visually impaired by making them 'see' the flavours through the aroma.

That was how the journey of *Vision of Palette*, the umbrella under which Chef conducted free cooking workshops for the visually impaired, began. And soon, what started at Selis Manor soon spread to the New York public library, the Braille libraries across New York and even at educational institutions like the New York and Princeton universities. That continued for a few months, and as the word spread, one day he found a film crew at one of the workshops he was conducting. They were there to film him for *NY1* (*New York One*), one of the most popular television channels in the state of New York.

'A few days later, on a Saturday morning, when I went to the house of one of the families I cooked for, the little girl in the house started jumping and shouting as she tried to call her mom.'

She kept repeating the words, 'Mom, it is the same guy

from television!' till the lady stepped out, and that is when she told Chef that they had seen him on *NY1* and she also knew that he was the 'New Yorker of the Week'!

It was the first time in history that an Indian had been given that title. The achievement gave him a sense of immense pride, as it was a validation long due—a success of the gamble he had taken by jumping off the cliff, quitting his job and trying to fly with dreams for wings. But it did not change the pace at which he was trying to spread the joy.

When the terrible tsunami tragedy struck the southern parts of India and devastated huge tracts of land in Southeast Asia, he knew that he had to do something.

'It was the first time in my life when I could actually make a difference, and that is when SAKIV was born. While it actually stands for South Asian Kids' Infinite Vision, when a little girl of Indonesian descent told me that SAKIV was my name spelt backwards, the innocence in the way that she explained what it meant to her told me we had set out in the right direction. We had decided to be catalysts. Catalysts who would host charity events and the cheques that came from them would go to the causes we supported. Initially, our focus was on tsunami relief, but now our main focus at SAKIV is to create awareness about visual disorders in children in Southeast Asia.'

SAKIV continued its work and a few years later, while he was constantly trying to open doors for others, yet another opportunity struck at his own door. He was invited to host an annual gala at the illustrious Rubin Museum of Art in New York City.

'It all started when I was being "sold for one night" at a conference in the summer of 2007 hosted by SAJA, the South Asian Journalists Association. The deal was that I would cook a meal for four people at the home of highest bidder. I had no qualms about it because I had many friends who were members of the SAJA. I had agreed to be a part of that conference because I knew that the proceeds from the highest bidder could go a long way in helping those friends. But I had no idea about what was in store for me. I couldn't believe that Shelley Rubin, one of the founders of the Rubin's Museum of Art, emerged as the highest bidder. The museum was a private collection of beautiful Himalayan art, started by Shelly and her husband, Donald Rubin. I had been a fan of it for quite a long time.

'I remember my first tryst with the museum. I had gone to see some artefacts they were displaying. The exhibition was called "I See No Strangers", from a quote by Guru Nanak Dev, the founder of Sikhism, when he spoke about how he felt that everyone was a part of him and that there was no discrimination on the basis of caste, colour or creed. The entire exhibit was a celebration of the heritage of Sikh religion.

'I didn't know how the stars had connected, but I knew that something magical was at play. I was ready to do my bit for the family who was and is doing so much to preserve our culture. Debra Morris headed the team that was going to organise the dinner at Shelley's house, and soon a dinner for four had taken the shape of a much larger get-together of connoisseurs of art and culture. The dinner that my team and I organised was inspired by the influence of Indian food around the world with a focus on the food from India, especially prepared for Christmas celebrations across the country. I had chosen Christmas even when the festival was still a while away because the Rubins had a tradition of setting up a Christmas tree and decorating it much before the actual festivities began. And while I was interacting with Shelley for the first time, she asked me if I would like to host the annual gala at their museum.'

The Nine Rivers Gala that is held every year at the RMA is one of the most popular events in New York City. It is a sit-down dinner and has had speakers ranging from reigning presidents of America to literary greats and famous artists.

Autumn, which is normally when the gala is held every year, was earmarked for the occasion in 2007 too. But the day was special for Chef, when it finally arrived, amid the effervescent glow of the candles, black coats and flowing gowns that moved across the room in the museum where the gala was being held, there were white chef coats floating all around the room.

Food has always been a very important part of human history and culture, and the museum, which is a celebration of the Himalayan art and culture, has always given it its due. That was why Chef had been chosen by the Rubins to head the team that was going to bring that culture to the tables of the guests at the gala which is a tribute to the great rivers that originate from the 'abode of the snow', the Himalayas.

And such was the resonance of the museum and what it stood for that Chef continues to be associated with them in multitude of ways.

'I'm always there for Shelly and Donald. I've always tried to further the cause of promotion of cultural heritages, whether it is from India or any other part of the world, and I'm in awe of what the Rubin's Museum of Art is doing. It is my privilege and the kindness of the Rubins that I've been given the reins of the Café at the museum. It is one of my favourite projects and the menu reflects the learning that I've had during my travels in the Himalayas. Each time I go there, I learn something new and the menu keeps evolving.'

And these travels even peeped out and greeted people in his food at *Junoon*. But it was one dish on that menu that made everyone sit up and notice, including Martha Stewart, when she saw Chef cook it when he was on *The Martha Stewart Show*—the Tree of Life.

The cauliflower cut vertically from the centre, rubbed with a blend of the choicest of Himalayan spices and made to sit on a bed of a Nepalese sauce of roasted tomatoes after it was roasted and shallow fried, brought out the vision of Chef—the beauty in the fusion of various food cultures from the east into the plates and palates of the West to create a beautiful tree that only knew the joy of giving.

The tree of life that had started with enhancing the lives of others at Selis Manor, continued to grow as Chef extended his support to causes such as the Amar Jyoti Centre for differently-abled kids that is run by Uma Tuli in Delhi; the importance of food in culture; and promoting a change in the way the society thinks about patriarchy by endorsing the '*Nayi Soch*' i.e., 'a new thought process' campaign.

He also works with Smile Foundation and represents the cause of 'Nutrition for Education' to aid the underprivileged kids in India, on a global platform. The idea behind this endeavour is to educate people everywhere about how important nutrition is for the children to be able to get a good education. He has taken a pledge of #MillionDollar4Nutrition to try and help make a difference in the lives of the malnourished kids in India. And since he believes in the balance of breaks, he has also pledged to take help of his epic about Indian festivals, *Utsav*, and use the proceeds from the sales of the first copy of the book to help the underprivileged kids in India celebrate festivals.

During his interactions with His Holiness the Dalai Lama during the shooting of his documentary, *Holy Kitchens*, which explores the traditions of food sharing through a spiritual prism, His Holiness started with a prayer that spoke about the sacrifice of each grain as it gives nourishment to us. And the words that His Holiness ended the prayer with stayed with Chef forever.

'Each one of us has a potential to make a better world.'

THE WINDOW OF JAMES BEARD

Faith is taking the first step even when
you can't see the whole staircase.
—Martin Luther King Jr

There is a window in the building that was used as a prison during the time of the Mughals in India that overlooks the Taj Mahal. It is believed that Shah Jahan, the Mughal Emperor who got the Taj Mahal built, requested his son and successor, Aurangzeb, to house him in a prison cell from where he could see the structure and stay close to his beloved wife, Mumtaz Mahal.

Windows are funny objects. They give a feeling of closeness, a breath of freedom and even a peek into one's soul if one looks carefully. And then, there are certain windows which are like unicorns. They're mythical and tales are woven around them. Only those who are brave enough to take the leap and set their imagination on fire, can enjoy the view that these windows have to offer.

One such window that has inspired many generations of chefs across continents is the window of the James Beard House.

While working for an Indian restaurant, *Diwan Curry House*, in Upper West Side, Chef also used to distribute flyers for various restaurants. One day, as he was sitting at one of his favourite places in New York, the memorial dedicated to John Lennon with the *Imagine* mosaic at the heart of it, he began to read one of the flyers in his hand.

'It had the same, clichéd menu that had been served for years. There was no change, no imagination, no risk, nothing. Imagination is difficult because imagination is risky. Imagination means risking alienating yourself from the way things have been done for years, and no one wants to be alienated. And there I was, sitting in front of the person who had written this beautiful song on imagination.'

That day, he decided he did not want to be the person who did not take any risks. He had come to America with a dream, the dream of becoming a Michelin-starred chef, and that dream wasn't going to be fulfilled by letting his imagination be trampled by the fear of failing.

He finished his job of distributing the flyers that evening, all the while his mind trying to figure out what he was going to do with the menu of *Diwan Curry House*, the restaurant where he worked. The next day he spoke to the management about how he wanted to introduce certain innovative items in the menu. And considering the imagination that had sparked the idea, it was decided that the risk would be taken.

Though that restaurant closed shortly, the spark of imagination never died. When he started working at *Salaam Bombay* in *Tribeca*, he introduced a few items in the menu. One of those items was a *gulkand-elaichi*-flavoured ice cream served in a bowl—a bowl made out of ice. Soon enough, the innovations began to get noticed. One day, Chef was presented with a request that left him surprised. One of the patrons loved the ice cream so much that she wanted to meet the person who had made it. And when she met him, she had yet another suggestion that had left him astonished yet another time in the span of a few minutes—she proposed that he should cook at the Beard House and even went on to recommend him to them.

When Chef heard the name of James Beard, the father of the American cuisine, his curiosity was piqued. That night, he researched it and found out that the Beard House was a continuity of the legacy that the great man had left behind. Cooking there was akin to cooking at the Governor's Ball at the Oscars! During that research, he came across a picture taken from a window of the kitchen of the Beard House. He felt that New York looked different from that window—a tad brighter, a whole lot swankier and even a little more home. He knew he had to grab the opportunity after what felt like a lifetime of struggles in New York.

Everything was set and in a few days he found the door of the elevator in an office on the 167 West 12th Street in New York opening to see an elderly woman who introduced herself as Arlyn Blake. Her empathetic eyes and warmth made Chef feel at ease immediately. What she told him during the conversation made Chef smile even more—'We always need Indian chefs; India is going to be the next big thing.'

Arlyn too remembers that day fondly.

'It all started one day, about fourteen years ago, when a young man walked into my office at the James Beard Foundation. Think earnest, clean-cut, well-spoken, young, innocent meets tough, old, New York Type A Feminist. He was a sort of skinny, really innocent youth, but in a few minutes I knew I had met a special person, a very strong, genuine person, who was going to make this world a better place.'

She asked him to prepare a menu for the dinner, but he had no idea what he could serve, and the research online only confused him more. So, he went with his gut feeling and risked a menu that was an eclectic blend of modern and traditional Indian food. After that, it was a nerve-racking wait of a few months, but when Arlyn's call came, it was imprinted on Chef's heart.

'This is Arlyn Blake, your Jewish mother. I want to let you know that on 23 August 2004, we've booked a dinner space for you. If you want to do it, let me know. But I must tell you that even if you don't, you're still my champion.'

The dinner was still about three months away. While it

meant little time to prepare, it was also a long and even more nerve-racking wait for the moment to arrive; a moment that was dotted with a lot more firsts for Chef.

A few weeks later, Arlyn called him: 'Son, I wanted to tell you that the calendar has come and I need your headshot.'

Till that day in his life, the only photograph of him that anyone had needed was the one that he had in his passport. He thought it was only movie stars and politicians who needed headshots. He had never heard that even chefs needed their pictures taken.

The summer of 2004 was setting in, but Arlyn's words felt like spring to Chef.

He shook the initial surprise off and spoke to Dorothy Shi, who was a regular at *Salaam Bombay*. Her quirky website 'shishotme' had got his attention when he found out what Dorothy did. He knew she would be able to help him get over his initial camera-shyness. And while doing the shots, when she asked him to put his hand on his chin, he asked if chefs needed headshots at all. It was an entirely new, somewhat awkward experience for Chef, but life as he knew it was changing and all he could do was play along.

Before that momentous day in *Salaam Bombay*, people who had eaten the food that he had made all his life had never requested to meet him, but afterwards, there was no looking back. After the final course at the Beard House, which was the same *gulkand-elaichi*-flavoured ice cream served in a frozen bowl of ice and rose petals, Chef and his team members were asked to go to the main dining area. He was a little apprehensive because he thought he had messed something up and they had called him to reprimand him. But when the team made it upstairs to the dining hall quietly, they were greeted with a standing ovation. That was the first time when someone had stood up and applauded Chef for his work. And then, he was also presented with a Wüsthof knife set, which is a present he treasures to this day. And the series of firsts continued when, as per tradition, he was asked to sign on an apron that had signatures of legends like Chef Daniel Boulud, Chef Eric Ripert, Chef Thomas Keller, Chef David Waltuck and many more who had shaped the way the world dines every day.

With a black marker in hand, Chef signed the apron, but he did so below the names of the others whom he considers to be people who have influenced his cooking. And then, he 'left' a piece of his heart in the Beard House in the form of a small heart that he drew right under his signature.

Before that evening on 23 August 2004, every time Chef walked by the James Beard House on the 12th Street, he saw the knives and the ladles looking back at him from the window. And during each of those times, his dream got stronger. The view from the James Beard House's window had taken many years in the making, but it was only the beginning of the rest of his life.

THE ENDLESS JOURNEY OF
1 MINUTE 30 SECONDS

Some people never go crazy.
What truly horrible lives they must lead.
—Charles Bukowski

'It was one o'clock in the afternoon on 4 October 2011. When I had woken up that grey, wintery morning, I had no clue what the day had in store for me. You never wake up knowing that life as you know it is going to change forever, right? I was in the kitchen when the hostess told me through the kitchen window that there was a call for me. I asked her if she could connect it to the kitchen's phone. She said that she could not because the "kitchen brats" had broken the phone there yet again. The kitchen phone had never worked because the kitchen was full of heightened emotions; every shift brought its own challenges. Each time we got the phone fixed, someone would vent their frustration on it. I think it used to quiver each time we got it fixed, waiting for the inevitable.

'I laughed and reminded her that I had got the phone that very morning. So, as I answered the call after she had transferred it, I heard a lady speak over the phone. I asked her who was on the line, but nothing could have prepared me for that lady's answer.

'She told me that it was a call from *The Michelin Guide*.

'I was running the service counter in the kitchen at that time, trying to expedite the lunch service. I handed the charge over, washed my hands and began walking to my office. It took me about a minute and thirty seconds to reach there from the kitchen, and through that entire "journey", my life flashed before my eyes. That yelling, those screams, the pain, the threatening, the bullying, the joys, that cool breeze that hit my face on a hot summer day at home, the travels, the people who backstabbed me and those who nurtured me; within those one-and-a-half minutes, I relived my entire life.

'I was walking down the steps where I sit and eat, and passing by the part of the kitchen where the pastry chefs were making their regular petit fours. I still remember the smell of the chocolate that they were tempering. And on my right, a guy passed me as he was carrying a big box of rice to the kitchen.

'Finally, when I reached the phone and spoke to the lady on the other side, the line was not clear. But I could hear the poise in her voice. She asked about how my day was going. I wanted to tell her about all my fears of being thrown out of the country, the threats and "burials" in my life, the fear of living in darkness and the joy of the surprising lights and constant evolution that I had gone through to reach that point where I was talking to her. But I settled for telling her that my day was going fine.

'She asked me how the restaurant was doing, other things I was working on apart from the restaurant and wished me luck for *Utsav* when I told her about it.

'While talking to her, I was looking at the noticeboard in the office that preserved a few significant memories I had brought with me from Amritsar. The constant struggle of many decades—almost half of my life, the sacrifices by my parents to be able to send me to America by never eating out or going on holidays, and not even buying new clothes, but ensuring that their children got all of that and more. Each of those memories was coming to my mind as I nodded absent-mindedly.

'The board also had a small, crumpled piece of old paper that I had found a few years ago. I think it was at the beginning of the winter of 2001 when I had found it and read the Mexican proverb that it had.

'"They came to bury us, but they forgot that we were seeds."

'The paper was crumpled because it had travelled with me everywhere I went ever since the day I found it, and it was present on all the noticeboards of the restaurants where

I worked. A person who has spent all his life trekking in the Himalayas might forget how much he has travelled, but when he looks at the sole of his shoes, it reminds him of the journey that he has undertaken, and all the things that he has left behind in his pursuit of happiness.

'That small piece of paper was reminding me of my entire journey as I was talking to that stranger. Due to the protocol, we are not even allowed to ask them their name, but she could sense that a lot was going on in my mind and asked me if I was fine.

'She tried to lighten the mood a bit, and then she said something that is etched in my memory for life.

'"Chef Vikas Khanna, from today you will be known as Michelin Star Chef Vikas Khanna."

'I did not respond to her. I know, I should have thanked her, but I was too numb. Sometimes, when it rains after a long drought, the farmers don't react much because they've waited for so long that they have no energy left to appreciate and enjoy the smell of the rain. All that they can manage is a smile.

'I went back up. The staff was eager to know about the conversation. One of the guys at the bar was even ready with a champagne bottle.

'But I was still too numb. I went to the staff restroom. After locking it from inside, I sat on the floor and cried like a child. Tears flowed down my cheeks as I repeated "Thank you, Mumma. Thank You, Papa" like a chant. I kept saying "thank you" to the ones who had helped me get there, to those who had pushed me against the wall and even those who had told me I wasn't meant to be there. I was born again that day and I thanked everyone for that reincarnation.

'As I finally walked out, my staff sprayed champagne on me. Andrew Blackmore, my friend, came and hugged me. He told me that from the moment he had seen me on Gordon Ramsay's *Kitchen Nightmares*, he could see that I listened to my heart.

'I remember how the phones started ringing and things began to change slowly after that call with a stranger.

'Our brain is funny, sometimes. Why is it that sometimes it is very lazy, and sometimes it remembers each and every detail of a particular moment? For example, almost everyone I know remembers the moment when they first heard about the attacks on 9/11. They remember what they were doing, what they were eating, where they were, everything.

'For me, this was a moment that stays frozen in time. This was something I had waited for more than twenty years.'

During his days in Manipal when he was studying at WGSHA, after reading an article which spoke about *The Michelin Guide*, Chef had told his mentor, Professor YG Tharakan, that he would work towards winning a Michelin star one day. But little did he or his mentor know about what destiny had in store for him as Tharakan Sir had smiled.

'You cannot buy a Michelin star, but keep working because that's when miracles happen,' he had replied.

Very few things make Chef smile. The very mention of his mother, Bindu Khanna; the thoughts of the food that *Biji* cooked; the day he held his niece, Ojasvi, for the first time; or the day when one-year-old Saumya walked out of the JFK airport to hug him. And the time when he and his father, Mr Davinder Khanna, had tears in their eyes as Davinder Ji was leaving for Amritsar after dropping him off in Manipal to begin his studies at his college. The memories bring a smile to Chef's face each time he remembers those moments.

And on 4 October 2011, another miracle got added to that list—the endless journey of one minute, thirty seconds.

THE WHITE HOUSE

*All our dreams can come true if we have the
courage to pursue them.*
—Walt Disney

There are some special moments that change the course of our lives forever. And then there are some exceptional pearls of joy whose soothing music, breathtaking views, and their very mention makes us smile. These pearls shine light on us till the day we leave this plane of life.

'On 24 August 2004, the day after I cooked at the Beard House, I gave notice at *Salaam Bombay*. I had come to America with a dream in my heart and that dream had been set ablaze. It was as if Mr Beard himself was encouraging me to begin a new chapter in my life—a chapter where my dreams were going to turn into a reality.'

Dreams are essential; they motivate us.

Chef's dream had been planted in his mind when Nishant, his elder brother, gifted him a copy of *Jonathan Livingston Seagull* and told him to fly and follow his own heart in the kitchens not just in India, but across the world.

'I told the guy who was taking my visa interview that America was the place that could brush me up and give me a new home where I could represent my original home. I told him that I felt as though another life was waiting for me there. And I remember that as he stamped my visa, he told me that he agreed with me and a life was indeed waiting for me in America.'

But it had not been smooth sailing for Chef in America in the initial days.

After moving to America on 2 December 2000 with a basket full of dreams, Chef had hoped to take off from where he had left—a successful catering business in his hometown. But he had no stable jobs waiting for him, no godfathers to hold his hand and the colour of his skin being more important than his skill in the kitchen, led him to harsh realities.

Each time Chef hears a Christmas carol, he is reminded of the chilly day in New York City. A few days before Christmas in the year 2001, Chef realised that he only had three dollars in his pocket. He decided to use half that money to eat a burger and the remaining half to get to work the next morning in the subway. But when he reached his workplace he realised that his employers had forgotten to inform him that the deli was closed that day. With no money in his pocket, he had begun walking back home when he spotted a queue. The queue was a few homeless people waiting to get into the New York Rescue Mission to escape the harsh New York winters.

'I stood in the queue and a kind soul at the entrance offered me a blanket. It was the first kind thing that someone had done for me in weeks. In that moment I realised that the story of the seagull was great, but only in the world of books. In reality, there was nothing like flying high like the seagull did. I felt like there was no place for me in America.'

That was the first time that the thought of going back home and to Lawrence Garden crossed his mind.

'I was lost. I did not know the direction that could have led to a change, and that is when I decided to go to the library on the 42nd Street and 5th Avenue. Many curious minds were sitting there, just reading. The amount of literature America has to offer to those who want to read is astounding. All you need to find is a way to reach the door of a library. The rest is taken care of by an identity card. And finding your way in New York, too, is very easy because the city was made by immigrants and they wanted to make numbering and naming easy for all the new settlers. If you're on 34th street, then 35th street is uptown; the first avenue is in the east, and tenth avenue is towards the west.

'Before that day, I had been doing various odd jobs and had been broke multiple times. I had no idea where to start, but that day when I reached the door of the library, I realised how easy it was to read the map and directions of the ways of life in the crazy city that New York is. It was that day when I realised that I needed to study and find a stable job.'

And when a stable job came by in the form of work at an Indian restaurant called *Salaam Bombay*, he also focused on studying. It was summer in 2001 when he managed to get into the Culinary Institute of America for a summer course.

Delores Custer, a New York resident for thirty-five years, recalls: 'I first met Vikas when he was working as a chef in *Salaam Bombay*. As we talked, he indicated that he was interested in learning about what I did. I told him that I took classes at the Culinary Institute of America just north of the city.'

Delores helped Chef with the admission formalities and when he got into the college, she helped him with the brushing up of the knowledge that he had collected over the years before coming to America. She also conducted an on-camera interview, helped him write recipes, and prepared him for cooking demos. She knew how invaluable these skills are for any individual in the hospitality industry, and when she saw the enthusiasm of Chef, it only encouraged her to teach him more.

'There was this assignment we had soon after I discovered the names Simon and Garfunkel. Their *Bridge Over Troubled Waters* had inspired me ever since childhood when I used to hear their songs on a little faceless magnetic tape that I had. I did not know their names back then because there was no internet to find out what had been inspiring me, but when I found out their names after listening to my roommate in CIA play their music in our dorm, I was ecstatic. I spoke about how I felt after finding out their names in the assignment which was an "interview" of thirty minutes where we had to speak about what inspired us to cook. Our entire conversation with Delores and the rest of the class was recorded. The purpose of that exercise was to show us how our expressions were when we spoke in a tense situation and help us rid ourselves of the fear of public speaking. It was important because the college saw us as potential entrepreneurs in the hospitality industry and made us perfect in the art of presenting ourselves in public.'

The grooming under the watchful eyes of Delores and other professors at the college helped Chef to continue on the path he had always had in mind. Even his penchant for taking risks in the creative realms was revived and it soon saw him venture out on a new journey with a restaurant called *Tandoor Palace*, where all the training of various years got wings of the American freedom of thought.

And it paid off.

His work at *Tandoor Palace* was noticed by many and it led to the doors of the hallowed world of television open up to him.

Being featured on *Kitchen Nightmares* on 8 April 2007 as a consultant chef at the restaurant, *Purnima*, led to a lot of international acclaim. Many new pinnacles, in the form of opportunities to be a part of other television shows across the world, being a host of *MasterChef India*, and signing new book deals, came Chef's way.

And it continued in no less than a fairy tale fashion—he landed in the White House, as the host of a conference to promote Indian culture and its spirit of giving.

'I had met Anju Bhargava, who was a member of Former President Barack Obama's "Advisory Council of Faith-Based and Neighborhood Partnership", many years ago when she spoke about the word *seva* in my documentary, *Holy Kitchens*. For her the word meant much more than its literal meaning of service. She felt that it was synonymous with spirituality. I connected with the way she was bringing India and her spiritual and cultural philosophies to the world. And when she was working on the plan to host a dinner at the White House for the American Hindu Seva Charities Conference to promote India and her spirit of *seva* and giving early in 2011, she got in touch with me.'

On 29 July 2011, Anju and Chef hosted a lunch with the theme of Street Food of India, and a dinner with a *satvik* theme at the conference. *Satvik* is a Sanskrit word that translates to 'pure and virtuous'. It is a philosophy that Chef tries to adopt in this food, and it was also one of the topics in his documentary, *Holy Kitchens*, that was showcased at the conference.

This was one of the major victories for Indian cuisine as it was applauded on a truly global platform for its sacred appeal. India's soft power resonated with all the attendees. And it even led to Chef being invited to the Thanksgiving Dinner that was hosted by the Obamas in New York in 2011.

His tryst with the Obamas continued as he was put in charge of the team that cooked at a fundraiser hosted for President Obama at the Rubin's Museum of Art on 14 May 2012. And he met them again when he got the opportunity to present a copy of his magnum opus about India, *Utsav*, to President Obama at the White House in August 2015.

Chef also got the opportunity to present copies of *Utsav* to His Holiness Pope Francis, His Holiness the Dalai Lama, Indian Prime Minister Narendra Modi, Her Majesty Queen Elizabeth II, Former President Bill Clinton, Senator Hilary Clinton, Mark Zuckerberg, and the Former Secretary-General of the United Nations, Ban Ki-moon.

Chef often says, 'When it rains, it pours. You just have to weather the storm.'

THE SEAGULL FOUND HIS HOME

*Have the courage to follow your heart and intuition. They
somehow know what you truly want to become.*
—Steve Jobs

As the team of Star TV heading the second season of
MasterChef India sat in the boardroom and deliberated
about the possible members of the panel of judges, early
in 2011, a new name came up—the name of Chef Vikas
Khanna.

Ever since the fire had been ignited from the time when
Chef appeared on *Kitchen Nightmares* in the spring of 2007 as
a consultant chef at the restaurant *Purnima*, it had started to
spread. Soon after being on the show with Gordon Ramsay
for the first time, he was called back to open the next season
of *Kitchen Nightmares*, where Gordon wanted to revisit one of
the biggest success stories of the show—*Purnima*.

Gordon's praise for the tasting menu that Chef had cooked specially for the show was as lavish as the food. He went on to say on television that 'the food that I have had at *Purnima* today is the best Indian food that I've ever had in my life and that includes what I've had in England too. In a way, I'm proud of Vikas's journey because I'm a part of it, but it is also hurting me a bit to think that New York is going to be the new global centre of Indian food in Vikas's hands.'

The words of the legend echoed in the minds of the millions who had tuned in to the show at prime time, and it put Chef on the map. The second appearance on Gordon's show was followed by television appearances in shows with high ratings, such as the season finale of *Hell's Kitchen, Throwdown with Bobby Flay* and *The Martha Stewart Show*.

'I got the first show by mistake, I think, but then the stroke of luck continued,' says Chef.

But Hiroko Kiiffner feels differently, 'Soon after the foodie website, *Eater*, had run a poll and announced that Vikas was "New York's Hottest Chef", a media frenzy led by bloggers and press erupted. An ethnic chef with such star power was newsworthy. Who was he and where had he come from? Young admirers came from everywhere, hoping to catch a glimpse of Vikas in New York.'

Coverage in the NY media then attracted the attention of the press in India. In a matter of weeks, their representatives, including executives from the popular television programme, *MasterChef India*, came to interview Vikas and, as they say, the rest is history. A few keystrokes, and the power of the internet had started Vikas's return to his home.'

But when it was time for homecoming, Chef was nervous.

Ruchi Shrivastava was one of the senior members of the team that was put in charge by Star TV Network to produce the first season of *MasterChef India*.

'At that time, in 2010, not many know that Vikas's name had come up for the first season of *MasterChef India* and we had asked him to send a video clip of himself talking about his work in America and other generic stuff. We wanted to see what his diction was like and if he would work for television. But when he sent the video, it was grainy and the sound was bad. We couldn't hear anything properly. We were pleasantly surprised to see how connected Vikas was to India. Because he had been living in America for many years, some of the team members were expecting him to speak with an American accent, but on the contrary, when he spoke Hindi, it still had a strong Punjabi accent. We knew that he could connect with audiences not just in India but across the globe.

'But since the video was not up to the mark, we were sceptical. It was the first ever season of *MasterChef* in India, and we wanted names that would have justified our stance that India, too, needed a franchise of the global phenomenon. We did not want to take a chance, which was why somehow his name was dropped from the list of possible judges for the first season.'

Maybe, it was just not meant to be at that time. Chef recalls, 'That day, I was tired and returning from a long shoot and recipe-testing for my book, *Khanna Sutra*, and had to record the clip while I was on the move. New York did not want me to leave for India, maybe.'

But Chef kept forging ahead in America and as the television appearances and other milestones continued, his name came up for discussion once again, early in 2011.

Ruchi recalls that, 'Vikas's name came up again in the second season because at that time we were looking for someone to fill Akshay Kumar's shoes. There was no direct comparison between both of them because one is a movie star and the other is a celebrated chef, but we needed someone who was as good-looking as Akshay, if not more, and Vikas fitted the bill. All of us felt that Vikas was going to be able to do justice to it because we had seen him on other shows in America and all of us loved his screen presence. So, this time we decided to meet him and have him audition in Mumbai. And after that had happened, the Punjabi accent in his Hindi and even the way he said "MasterChef" with an American-Punjabi accent, had become a huge bone of contention for everyone. A lot of us put our jobs at stake as we invested faith in his knowledge and passion for food.'

But that meant that the burden of expectations was squarely sitting on Chef's head. And he was well aware of that.

Television in America was very different because, while millions watched him, they knew him and they knew how he had brought Indian food and culture to America. But in India, where not many knew about him and his work in America, he had to prove himself all over again. A much larger number of people watched him. It only added to the burden.

But the production team put their faith in him and used all their weight to help him through the initial days of nervousness.

When it was time for his first appearance on *MasterChef India*, during the shoot of the premiere episode in Vizag, Ruchi remembers, 'After he was welcomed by the other judges, Chef Kunal Kapoor and Chef Ajay Chopra, he greeted the contestants in a loud voice, much to their delight. But then, Vikas lost his voice. He was so nervous that he simply choked. We realised what had happened, and immediately, all of us at the set rallied behind him. A technical break was announced to the contestants. Vikas was helped through the bout of anxiety by the crew members as well as his fellow judges and we managed to complete the shoot.'

Many believe that in the world of spotlights and cameras, it is easy to buckle under the pressure and even lose track of reality. The hectic schedules, short shelf lives and the constantly roving eyes of the public and the media can lead to burnouts. All this leads to everyone finding their own ways to retain their sanity—some sort of grounding factor. And for Chef, it has been his mother.

During the entire Season 2 of *MasterChef India*, his guardian angel was always there, not saying anything, but her omnipresent blessings helped Chef power through it all.

Under the watchful eye of his mother and the constant encouragement from everyone, Chef stuck it out while constantly working on his diction.

Kapil Motwani, who was on the team of Star TV, the channel that was producing the show, remembers that 'Samar Sir, a Hindi diction expert, was given the charge of helping Chef refine his Hindi pronunciations and reduce the influence of Punjabi in the way he spoke. Hindi was the main language of the show and we needed all the judges to be fluent in it.'

But none of the training worked on Chef.

'We realised later that it was our good fortune that none of the diction training worked. People loved Vikas because he spoke from his heart and that accent helped the people watching him on their television feel like they were talking to someone real,' Kapil Motwani shares. It was corroborated by the ratings of the show.

Chef appeared on Indian television for the first time on 22 October 2011 when Season 2 of *MasterChef India* was telecast. And the stand of the production team was vindicated as the audience showed their love for the 'good-looking Indian Chef from America' who used little phrases like '*Rab rakha*', which means 'May God be with you', and '*koi nai, koi nai*', which loosely translates into 'It is okay, don't worry', while trying to allay the fears of nervous contestants. The little Punjabi phrases made the audiences see the real face of Chef through the cameras and as the show went on from the second to the third and fourth seasons, the audience as well as the contestants started seeing him as a 'nurturer'—almost like a parent.

And the audience's love led him to start hosting Fox Network's *Twist of Taste* after the first appearance in the third season in January 2014. He also appeared in a feature on *MasterChef Australia* as a guest judge in an episode in June 2014; and hosted *Mega Kitchens* on National Geographic in June 2015.

'Oprah was the one who taught everyone how the power of television could be used to create a difference in people's lives. It struck a chord with me. Ever since I started doing television shows, I've tried to make sure that instead of allowing television to use me, I use it to spread the food culture and celebrations around. When I went to Australia, I had decided that I was going to make rendered duck breast with steamed rice cakes and a few other condiments. But they told me they wanted a more challenging dish that also reflected something I stood for. I knew that I had to do something that would take people to India through the flavours. That was why I chose to make my version of *chicken tikka masala*, which is one dish that people in the West relate with India, but I did it with flavours of my own. A piece of chicken breast with fig stuffing was cooked using the sous-vide technique, where I used steam to cook the meat instead of the traditional way of searing the meat using the heat of a tandoor. I accompanied that with a Madrasi-style chutney that was an ode to the flavours of Chennai; and crispy rice *pappadams* (feather-light rice sheets) to go with the chicken. I wanted to use the platform that I was given to show the people across the world that Indian food too can look and smell beautiful. I've always been very careful about what I say on television because words are powerful, and when someone uses them without putting much thought into it, they can affect the lives of millions.'

And this is something that has been hailed by his peers.

Celebrated chef, Bobby Flay, who Chef Vikas has worked with on American television, feels that, 'Vikas is an American treasure lent to us by his native India.' Legendary American chef, Eric Ripert, with whom Chef Vikas has worked on multiple occasions, including the times when they have collaborated at the Rubin's Museum of Art in New York, says, 'Vikas has gone on a very large scale to bring India to the World.' And back in India, Chef Manish Mehrotra, known for taking Indian cuisine to great heights himself, feels, 'Vikas's work on television, in books, through talks and all other media, is helping all of us get closer to our goal of taking Indian cuisine to the levels that cuisines from countries like Japan and Italy enjoy.'

Chef recalls that 'my brother, Nishant, gave me this book by Richard Bach, called *Jonathan Livingston Seagull*, which talks about a seagull who learnt how to fly. But he also told me that while the seagull came back home, he wanted me to go and spread my wings and the aroma of our culture everywhere in the world. Thank you, Mr Bach, because you are like the sun; you will never know the number of lives that you've nourished.'

AN UTSAV CALLED INDIA

You've the heart of India in your book, Utsav.
—**His Holiness Pope Francis**

Sometimes, even the most negative criticism can set off something so positive that it becomes a seven-coloured wonder in the midst of a balmy day.

A few years ago in America, someone told Chef that no matter how good his writing or skills were going to be, he was always going to be ten times lesser than a white-skinned person. For the first time in his life, Chef's confidence was shattered. But it also gave birth to a new wave of resilience that even he had not known before that point in his life.

He often connects this moment to a tiny seed, which is buried in darkness, that reincarnates by channelising its inner power.

That day Chef decided that he did not want to be equal

to others. He was ready to risk everything to be eleven times better and prove to everyone that India and her culture, and not the colour of the skin of Indians, mattered.

In that moment *Utsav* was born.

'One day, I will write the most expensive cookbook in the world,' he told himself.

When you send something out to the universe, it sends it back. Maybe, the form and the time is something that no one can predict, but it does come around in a full circle.

'Andrew Blackmore, my friend who helps me with my literature and kitchen, has been with me ever since I started working with him in *Purnima*. Before moving to *Purnima*, which was *Dillon's* when he had moved, he had worked in *Savoy*, which was one of the most well-recognised and respected restaurants in New York. His American sensibilities meshed perfectly with my vision for Indian food. And because he understands what I want to do for Indian food, he has helped me through many of the books I've published over the years.'

And what is interesting is that Andrew was also a part of the occasion when Chef met someone who changed his life forever.

'Andrew was also with me while hosting the *Nine Rivers Gala* at the Rubin's Museum of Art in the autumn of 2007. That is where I had the privilege of meeting Sir Salman Rushdie. He had recently been granted knighthood by Her Majesty Queen Elizabeth II and the smile on his face was speaking a language of its own. I remember him telling me that he felt my food was similar to poetry.'

Sir Rushdie recalls, 'I've known Vikas for many years. He cooked a spectacular feast for a party I gave about ten years ago and from that moment I knew his talent was something very special. Vikas's food is simple and has grace and humility but, at the same time, it is also extremely loud on creativity.'

Coming from one of the masters of the literary world, it carried a lot of weight. When he told Chef that he should try to tell the stories in his heart, having survived through the years with no godfather in America, the words were imprinted upon Chef's mind.

Sir Rushdie told Chef, 'You must have the skin of an elephant and the heart of a poet. There is no other way that you could have survived.'

The message has never left Chef's heart.

'And when I told him that I did write, but I didn't know if it was any good, he asked me to read some of my poetry to him. He told me that I must write more because we were in America and it was the land that loves free thoughts and has always welcomed new literature. He said the people here in America would appreciate that along with my food, I was also trying to bring my culture to them.'

Empowered by these words, Chef mustered courage to venture into yet another unchartered territory in his life—literature.

'There is a difference between what an author does and

what is done by a chef. A chef makes a dish and it is consumed; sometimes, it is retained in the memory and sometimes it is not. But a book has the power of immortality. You can take a picture of some food that is in the precise position and at the right temperature, and after that, when it starts to decay, it doesn't matter because you've immortalised it in the glory of its youth in that single frame. And you can actually enhance its glory by writing about its history, culture, traditions and rituals—a story that will be read even centuries from now, by someone who isn't born yet.'

Chef's first five books were self-published and existed in small networks in America. But this 'small' beginning also opened a door to a whole new world of flavours.

Hiroko Kiiffner, the 'lady in charge' at the Lake Isle Press in New York, was someone Chef had known for many years. She was known as the 'queen maker' of America because she was the one who introduced Rachel Ray and her thirty-minute cooking to the world in a grand yet subtle way through her publishing house.

Chef remembers that 'Rachel became a rage in America and the person who was standing strong with her was Hiroko. I knew I had to talk to her about this idea I had. It was in the year 2009. Thanksgiving was round the corner when I wrote an email to Hiroko. I also told her about *Flavors First*, a book I wanted to write because I felt that whenever one talked about food, it was always about the flavours that brought back memories. I wanted the book to be as much about food and flavours as it was about memories—my own memories that I wanted to talk about in the book along with various recipes.'

Chef had been turned down by many other publishers but Hiroko saw the passion in Chef's writing and she also saw how deeply infused the flavours of India were in each of his recipes and stories. She shares, 'He sees life writ large, charts his own path, while passionately celebrating the rich culture of India with the rest of the world,' which is why she decided to take a leap of faith and decided to publish *Flavors First*. Her faith was rewarded when the book won the Benjamin Franklin award in 2012 and was feted as one of the most well-crafted cookbooks. Later Hiroko also published Chef's book *Return to the Rivers*, which was highly acclaimed for bringing Himalayan cuisine and culture to the world, and was nominated for the prestigious James Beard Award.

And today, the count stands at thirty-four, out of which twenty-five have already been published, and the planning for the next five years is already in the works.

But one of these books is extra special for Chef. While he worked on books that covered different facets of Indian cuisine and culture, *Utsav* was always on his mind and in his heart.

'While managing the schedules between India and New York was crazy in itself, I added yet another element of craziness to the entire set of things that was close to my heart—*Utsav*. It was an inner calling, and my teams in America and India understood what I was trying to do. They knew that no matter how challenging it was going to be, we had to bring the book out. In 2004, when I put the proposal to an

American publisher for the first time, it was rejected. And that was followed by a barrage of rejections from various other publishers. Everyone said the same thing: India was not a subject significant enough to deserve a book on a very large scale. Each of those rejections was like a repetition of the remark that I was ten times less, and it only made my resolve stronger. I wanted to use all my energy and contacts that I had built over these years to create *Utsav*.'

Chef took thousands of pictures he had clicked during his travels across India, spread over more than eight years, filled a suitcase with copies of those images and sent it off to Suresh Gopal at Bloomsbury India's office in New Delhi. The office was in the process of being shifted to a larger space nearby and the only thing available in their existing place was a small desk. Chef managed to put the bag on it so that Suresh Ji and the entire team of Bloomsbury could see Chef's vision in the pictures. The desk was rickety, but proud to bear the weight of Indian culture upon it.

These were the times of film and not digital media. When Suresh Ji saw the images, he thought Chef wanted to do a book containing only pictures, but Chef told him about his plan to do a book which was an amalgamation of Indian culture in the form of pictures, recipes and information about festivals from all across India.

'I told Suresh Ji that the book was going to be my entire life's journey wrapped up in a few pages for everyone to see. I hoped people would fall in love with India all over again.'

They were sold. They agreed that this was a story that needed to be told the way Chef had imagined it. Suresh Ji said, 'The only way others will understand what we have in mind is through a dummy of the book.' That put a chain of actions in motion. A dummy was made with the vast collection of images Chef had brought so that it could be presented to the London and New York offices of Bloomsbury.

So, when Chef met Richard Charkin, the head of the Bloomsbury office in London, they chose a café in Chelsea, but when they began to go through the book, they forgot to order a meal! Richard told Chef, 'Going through this book is like falling in love with India all over again. The world has not seen India like this, and we need to change that. So, we are going to go ahead and do this. It is a risk, but it is a risk we've to take.'

And a similar story unfolded in New York when Chef met George Gibson, the head of Bloomsbury in New York. He, too, fell in love with the book and felt like this was the book that was going to change the perception that Indian books were cheap, in such a way that there would be no ceiling for books by Indian authors ever again.

What followed were many more years of extensive travel as Chef had his motivation renewed. He dived deep into the cultural fabric of India and left no stone unturned as he scoured the length and the breadth of the country researching ceremonies, rituals and festivals synonymous with the culture and the sacred essentials that were an inseparable part of these ancient traditions. Chef shot almost 90 per cent of the pictures himself. It was difficult to make it to every festival, but his inner calling kept motivating him. It took many years, but whether it was having to wake up at 3:00 in the morning to be in time for the early morning festivities of Pongal, the harvest festival of Tamil Nadu, or travelling for hours to a distant corner of the suburbs in Mumbai, only to capture the true essence of the lamp-lighting ceremony of the Jain religion—he never shied away and was always on time. And in the process, he spent many precious months and even got robbed in Delhi once, but none of it deterred him.

His team stood firmly behind him throughout.

Manisha Singh, one of the senior-most employees at Smile Foundation, the charity Chef represents as its global ambassador, remembers how he used to manage his time in India between shooting for *MasterChef India*, attending festivals for *Utsav*, and then squeezing in time to work for the tiny tots helped by Smile.

She says, 'The backbone of his team was his mother, Bindu Ji. Whenever Vikas was struggling for energy and motivation, Bindu Ji was there. And I know this because when I was pregnant with my son, Yug, she asked Chef to visit me at my home in Pune to get my blessings because she believed that a pregnant woman had the power of the universe in her being. She felt that if I blessed *Utsav*, it would rise to heights even he had not imagined. And he did exactly what she wanted him to do. After taking her blessings, he travelled for more than twenty-four hours and came to my home. But I know that more than anything else, he was excited about what my reaction would be on seeing *Utsav* for the first time.'

Armed with the power of the universe, Chef managed to spread his fire across the world. *Utsav* found a place in the memories of people and the libraries of visionaries across the world, such as His Holiness Pope Francis, the 266th Pope of the Roman Catholic Church, and His Holiness the Dalai Lama, the current spiritual leader of the Buddhist community across the globe; and world leaders like the current Indian Prime Minister, Narendra Modi; former American Presidents, Barack Obama and Bill Clinton; Former First Lady, Michelle Obama; Senator Hilary Clinton and most recently, Her Majesty Queen Elizabeth II.

But then, one thing was still left to be done before the spread of the fire was going to be complete—the homecoming.

Thousands of students and faculty members of Manipal's WGSHA and many of their friends and guests came together to witness this homecoming that was yet another milestone—the first public unveiling of *Utsav* anywhere in the world, right after it had set the world record for being the most expensive cookbook in the world after being auctioned for INR 30 lakh, or about USD 45,000 to Rashesh Kanakia of Mumbai. The word *utsav* means festival, and true to its name, the proceeds received from the auction of this special copy of *Utsav* will be given to Smile Foundation, and will be used to help underprivileged kids across India celebrate festivals.

Manipal has always been close to Chef's heart. This was the place where his passion for food received the arsenal to turn it into a career that has spanned across countless restaurants and countries over decades. And it will witness yet another ode to India from Chef—the first-ever kitchen museum in the world that will house thousands of pots, pans, rolling pins, ladles, bowls, spoons, forks, serving spoons, hand-cranked ice cream makers or, in other words, almost every piece of equipment from the history of India, and even various other parts of the world, that are an ode to our love for food.

'Every time I visit India, I carry a piece of India with me. But I always knew that for every piece of it I've taken, I was going to give back more, but not before I had multiplied it by thousands. *Utsav* was the first step in this direction, and the Culinary Museum is going to continue singing the ode, hopefully all through my lifetime and beyond. That is why I chose to unveil *Utsav* here, because where else could I possibly do this?'

And as the applause rang out to commemorate all the milestones achieved and the ones still to come, there was a little milestone that was being rewritten in Chef's heart—the journey from the remark of being less than the others to bringing the most expensive cookbook in the world to life and showcasing the wealth of Indian culture to everyone was complete.

THE MOONLIT KITCHENS

There is a voice that doesn't use words. Listen.
—Rumi

The band, Aerosmith, has been encouraging people to dream on till their dreams come true, since 1973. But sometimes, many of our dreams don't shape up into reality. And sometimes, they take a form different from what we had imagined.

'When I was preparing to cook at the Beard House along with my team, one person who inspired me at every step was Julia Child, a close friend of Mr Beard's, who had been instrumental in setting up the James Beard Foundation and the renovation of the house where Mr Beard lived, to transform it into a hall of fame for food. Julia brought the French cuisine to America and inspired a whole generation of cooks. But it was extremely difficult for me that a few days before I was to cook at the Beard House on 23 August 2004, she passed away. Julia always inspired me and still does. I had imagined cooking for her but, unfortunately, I missed the opportunity to meet her or cook for her. It hurts me even today when I think about it.'

Sometimes, dreams don't come true. But that doesn't mean one should stop dreaming. One of Chef's favourite songs, *Sunscreen*, by Baz Luhrmann says, 'Save your love letters, destroy your bank statements', and that is something which is ingrained in him. He saves the letters sent to him by those who love and respect him, and sometimes when he is feeling low while doing countless number of things, many of which are only out of love for the cause or the people associated with it, he picks up and reads those letters.

'The letters energise me and give me the power to move on and dream again. I get energy from people, and the people get energy from me; it is a constant circle.'

And they also help give birth to many new dreams.

In 2010, while shooting for his documentary, *Holy Kitchens*, Chef met Arun Gandhi, the visionary grandson of the Father of the Nation, Mohandas Karamchand Gandhi. During the conversations, Chef got to know about the love for eggplant that the Father of the Nation had, and the food restrictions that he imposed on himself. Chef wished he could have cooked for the Mahatma, who brought freedom to India and taught her children to dream. Unfortunately, that dream of cooking for the great man cannot come true, but Chef feels happy that he was able to cook a meal for his grandson and express his gratitude to the legacy of the Mahatma.

Another dream he hopes will come true one day is to be able to cook for his musical inspiration.

'If I ever had the power to unite people, I'd use it to convince Simon and Garfunkel, the geniuses who inspired my young mind in my sleepy hometown at a time when I didn't even know who they were. Those were the times of magnetic tapes, and I had gotten to know them through a complete stroke of luck as I had found an unmarked tape in my father's shop. We used to rent out video tapes, but somehow this little audio tape had made its way to us. And because no one in Amritsar knew anything about English music, my father let me have it thinking that I would get bored of it soon. But the exact opposite happened. Somehow, their music used to calm me down during all my struggles, and I hope to get the opportunity to use my food to bring some peace to them some day.'

Yet another dream involves the red carpet one more time. And no, it is not Cannes. After launching *Utsav*, at Cannes in 2015, now he dreams of feeding those who have hunger for the Golden Statuette, the legendary Oscar Award.

Once the hunger of a select few from the many talented ones is satisfied, all of them, right from the Oscar winners and nominees, to the presenters and performers, and glitterati from the political and business echelons, descend the red carpet after the awards' ceremony to satiate yet another hunger—the hunger for food and fun. While this after party, also known as the Governor's Ball, is hosted by the Governor of the Academy, the reins of the culinary preparations have been handled by Chef Wolfgang Puck for the past twenty-two years. Chef hopes that someday he and his team would get an opportunity to work along with Chef Puck to host the dinner at the Ball.

But, dreams and success are two different things. The definition of success, too, is different for every individual. Chef dreams of writing fifty books in his lifetime, and eventually let cooking and the kitchens take a backseat so that he can concentrate on the nutrition and education dreams of the world through his foundation, SAKIV. Being able to give back to the society and helping as many people in as many ways as possible is what he wants.

'Creativity is not bound by numbers. There is no reason behind deciding on the number fifty, but my heart says I must write and share my knowledge. But the fiftieth book will be the closure.

'There is no definition of success. For me, it is all about balance. I just have a few black T-shirts and chef coats. I don't own anything much. For me, success is not reflected in a bank statement. Yes, everyone has bills, but if you don't have to think much about them and you can sleep in the night with a few thoughts that make you smile and help you sleep, that is success. Despite being the brand ambassador for Mercedes, I couldn't buy a car made by them for my father. I consider that as the opposite of success. I never asked him if he wanted a Mercedes, which is why he never told me. It will stay with me forever. I realised that our parents never ask for anything, but give everything to us all their lives. One day, you might be able to buy them a fleet of cars, but you won't be able to buy time or turn it back. Family always comes first for me.

'If you wake up in the morning and are able to enjoy a perfect ripe peach or some freshly squeezed orange juice to help you start your day with a smile, that is success.'

Some of his dreams didn't come true and sometimes, some of his dreams that he had conceived with a lot of love and imagination, and then nurtured them over the years, were snatched away from him. But that doesn't stop him from enjoying that perfect peach whenever he has the opportunity to have one, or sitting in his kitchen as the moonlight streams in, thinking about *Biji* and the aromas in her kitchen when he was a young boy. In the words of the great Muhammad Ali, 'Don't count the days, make the days count.'

THE STARS ARE WAITING

There is no why.
—Philippe Petit

It was a grey, windy day in New York City in August 1974. A thin, wiry man clad in black stood still on a wire almost as thin as him. But the wire seemed to be connected to nothing, as it disappeared into a white abyss. And then, as if the heavens had a plan for him, the clouds parted, revealing one of the twin towers, about 200 feet away, to which the wire was attached.

This moment had taken many years of preparation, and many lies and favours later, it was time for the coup.

This twenty-four-year-old man's name was Philippe Petit. He was used to flirting with danger while putting his life on the line each time, literally. But that day, it was a new high for him as he walked eight times between the Twin Towers,

1350 feet off the ground and even posed for the awestruck onlookers of the financial district in New York. When he finally decided to stop (after being threatened by the cops who told him that they would loosen the tension between the high wires or pluck him from the sky with the help of a helicopter) and step off the wire, he was arrested. As he was being taken away for a psychiatric examination by the cops who thought he was crazy, someone asked him why he had tried this incredulous stunt.

'There is no why.' That is all that the Frenchman said with a smile.

Chef remembers, 'One morning, my manager asked me if I was delighted because of what had happened. I had no clue what he was talking about. But when he told me that Philippe had tweeted that I could cook for him whenever I wanted, I couldn't stop smiling. Philippe inspires me every day. And very soon, I'm going to find a way to fly to France with my team and cook for the man who taught me that there is no why.'

Chef also strives to be as much like his mother as possible.

'I'm Bindu Khanna,' he said recently, while proclaiming his love for his mother.

The bond that he shares with his mother translates into several incidents and stories. Sometimes, he expresses his love for her by proclaiming on social media that he is Bindu Khanna, and sometimes he breaks into a conversation with her right in the middle of a room full of people being fed his food.

The entire audience looked on that night at a charity dinner hosted by him for Smile Foundation, as he took the stage reluctantly because he wanted to use his time to ensure that the dinner service was smooth, rather than stepping on stage to talk. But when he did, he forgot he was on the stage and started talking to his mother sitting in the first row as he recalled an incident from his childhood.

There was a time when the family had a small shop in Basant Avenue in his hometown, named *Dillagi*. It was in the business of renting out video cassettes. There was one movie which Chef's father, Davinder Khanna, recommended to everyone—the story of a fighter named Rocky. As a young boy, Chef didn't understand why his father recommended it to everyone, and neither could he understand the influence this movie made in America had in the small, sleepy town in northern India. His father's enthusiasm about the movie often made him wonder if his father had invested money in it or if he was the official distributor for it.

'I keep pushing you because you're my Rocky,' his father used to tell him.

But Chef hated that movie because he had to cycle around the city in scorching heat to deliver this piece of inspiration to people and then collect it to set out to deliver it once again. The trips on the bicycle were never-ending and this led him to hate the movie so much that he promised himself that he would never watch it.

And he never did, till the day his father passed away on 31 January 2015.

After finishing the rituals in Amritsar, he didn't speak much while returning to New York. But as soon as he got back, the first thing he did was watch *Rocky*. He called his manager to tell him that he needed to watch *Rocky* in peace and asked him to cancel all his appointments and engagements for that day. After watching the movie twice, he went on to watch Sylvester Stallone's acceptance speech when the movie won the Oscar for the Best Picture in 1977.

Once when Chef was asked what his biggest achievement in life was, he said that it was the Oscar dedicated to him, because Stallone had dedicated the Academy Award to all the Rockies in the world.

'I don't know what my parents saw in me, but I was their Rocky and that Oscar was dedicated to me.'

Maybe he didn't know it, but his mother, who was sitting in front of him in the first row, knew. She said nothing, but her smile said everything. As the audience at the charity dinner and thousands on social media platforms heard him speak, they took it as a well-rehearsed speech, but only she knew that it was as if her son was having a conversation with her over the dinner table in their home in Amritsar, telling her about those hot, sweaty days from his childhood.

'Yes, I helped my father run our family business, and I'm not ashamed of my roots. You know why? Because a tree is only as strong as its roots and our business was where our roots were. It ensured that there was food on our plates every day.

And that very food and what we did back then is why I am here today.'

His commitment to his roots reflects in his instinctive and spiritual approach to ingredients and techniques he uses to create recipes. And that is how Chef hopes to continue working in the future, without ever questioning the why of things.

'There is no why. If you love something, you have to love it unapologetically, unconditionally and unfalteringly, no matter what. This is a common trait across spheres, whether it is an Olympian who has won a gold medal, or a Pulitzer-winning author, or a Michelin-starred chef. You cannot let anyone ask you why you're doing it. You do it because you love it and you see something that others cannot. And that is because you see with your heart and they see with their eyes. It is your dream and it will stay yours. You can live with it, bury it or you can nourish it into a tree.'

Many times in Chef's life people tried to pull him down, and bury him—sometimes by playing dirty games and sometimes with sharp words. And sometimes, even with mocking laughter—as when he hobbled into his classroom wearing special shoes that helped him walk as a five-year-old boy. Maybe, at that time, it was a little hurtful because he couldn't even take part in the games on the grounds of his school without being made fun of, but today he thanks them because that laughter gave him strength. Without them, he would have never known the resilience in himself.

'I thank the darkness because it made my life brighter.'

Every seed has to be buried in darkness at some point. Every mountain and every tree had a fear of being destroyed. Many times, they were. But then, they were reborn. Chef was destroyed several times while trying to take the risks that came along as a cost of reaching out for his dreams. But the resilience that he had found in his childhood stayed with him in those times, and he didn't stay buried; he always got back up.

Philippe's smile when he said simply that 'there is no why', as he was being whisked away by the cops, at the end of an iconic video clip that was shot by the shutterbugs while he was walking in his park 110 storeys off the ground, has stayed with Chef ever since he saw it. That triumphant smile helped him in times of darkness and destruction, and those words were what inspired many reincarnations and dreams, including *Utsav*, his culinary epic on Indian festivals.

During the unveiling of *Utsav* in India at his alma mater in Manipal in 2017, when Chef made his way towards the stage, the sounds of the hundreds of drums and the flames of the lamps welcomed him back home where it had all begun. Thousands of students cheered as life was turning a full circle, as the young boy who had come from Amritsar in an old pair of blue jeans and a checkered shirt with eyes full of dreams was coming back to Manipal in a sharp, black blazer. And as the sea of young minds that were seated in the gathering listened to him with eyes full of dreams, his mother's words that had set his mind ablaze time and again, came out dazzling:

'In the end, there is only one truth: the stars are waiting for you,' his mother had said. 'There will be people sitting on the other side of the moon, the dark side, trying to make everyone else stay with them on that side. Whether you decide to ask why and stay with them or decide to blossom and reach out for the stars, is up to you.'

GLOSSARY

1. *Mauli*—A red or vermillion-coloured thread tied around one's wrist in religious ceremonies.
2. *Biji*—Grandmother or a mother in some cases—in Punjabi. For Chef, *Biji* is a piece of his heart, his grandmother.
3. *Veer* Ji—A word used to refer to an elder brother with respect.
4. *Bua*—A Hindi/Punjabi word for the sister of one's father.
5. *Masoor Dal*—A yellow soup made with split orangish-pink lentils.
6. *Bauji*—A salutation in Punjabi, used to address one's father or grandfather.
7. Captain Imagination—Yes, it is a reference to 'Captain Planet', the cartoon character from the 1990s, who inspired many kids of that generation.
8. *Poha*—Flattened rice flakes, often eaten for breakfast or for a light snack in Indian homes.
9. *Rajma-Chawal*—A combination of a curry made out of red kidney beans and boiled rice.
10. *Gulkand*—A jam-like preserve made from dried rose petals.
11. *Elaichi*—Cardamom.

A HUMBLE SEED

Though you are today a lonely buried seed,
You feel you're lost in this whole stampede;
At the moment you feel, you're destroyed,
Life is busted and lost in a dark deep void;
Have little faith, this darkness will disappear,
Every greatest mountain had the same fear;
Soon you will be reincarnated into a tree,
Giving shades, fruits and nests to the free;
Don't let anyone bully and let your heart bleed,
You've all the courage you need, Oh lonely seed.

—Vikas Khanna

Little Viku being showered with love by his mother and aunt in Delhi after the surgery of his feet when he was just one month old.

Tikka ceremony at Chef's home in Amritsar when he was five years old.

Chef (second from left) celebrating his fourth birthday in Amritsar.

At a qawwali performance (third from right in the front row) at his school,
St Jude's School, in Amritsar in the fourth grade.

Chef in his first jacket at the age of ten in Amritsar; small victories.

Chef and his sister, Radhika, getting ready for their elder brother,
Nishant's wedding in Amritsar in 1997.

Chef with his parents at the Brooklyn Bridge when they visited him in
New York City for the first time in 2003.

Chef with his friend, Sandhya, who took him with her to
Mumbai in 1994 for her modelling assignment.

WGSHA days, Manipal, 1991.

Eid *mubarak*, Dubai, 2015.

Chef with President Barack Obama during a special meeting to present *Utsav* to him in New York in 2015.

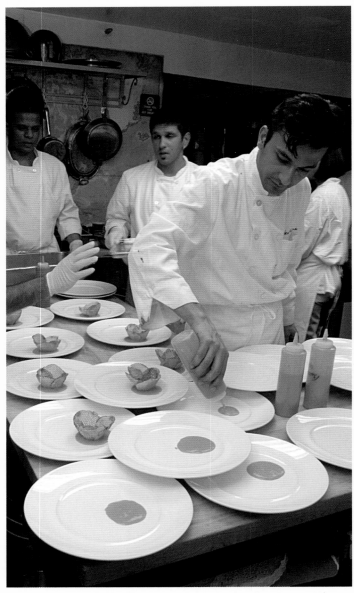

Chef cooking at the James Beard House in New York in August 2004.

A candid moment in the kitchen.

Chef with his nieces, Ojasvi and Saumya, in Amritsar in June 2008.